Rainer Eisfeld
Political Science: Reflecting on Concepts,
Demystifying Legends

Rainer Eisfeld

Political Science: Reflecting on Concepts, Demystifying Legends

With an Introduction by John Trent
(Former Secretary General,
International Political Science Association)

Barbara Budrich Publishers
Opladen • Berlin • Toronto 2016

A CIP catalogue record for this book is available from
Die Deutsche Bibliothek (The German Library)

© 2016 by Barbara Budrich Publishers, Opladen, Berlin & Toronto
www.barbara-budrich.net

ISBN   978-3-8474-0506-1 (Paperback)
eISBN   978-3-8474-0928-1 (eBook)

Das Werk einschließlich aller seiner Teile ist urheberrechtlich geschützt. Jede Verwertung außerhalb der engen Grenzen des Urheberrechtsgesetzes ist ohne Zustimmung des Verlages unzulässig und strafbar. Das gilt insbesondere für Vervielfältigungen, Übersetzungen, Mikroverfilmungen und die Einspeicherung und Verarbeitung in elektronischen Systemen.

Die Deutsche Bibliothek – CIP-Einheitsaufnahme
Ein Titeldatensatz für die Publikation ist bei der Deutschen Bibliothek erhältlich.

Verlag Barbara Budrich ⬤ Barbara Budrich Publishers
Stauffenbergstr. 7. D-51379 Leverkusen Opladen, Germany

86 Delma Drive. Toronto, ON M8W 4P6 Canada
www.barbara-budrich.net

Jacket illustration by Bettina Lehfeldt, Kleinmachnow
www.lehfeldtgraphic.de
Typesetting: R + S Beate Glaubitz, Leverkusen, Germany
Printed in Europe on acid-free paper by
paper&tinta, Warsaw

Contents

Peenemünde: Challenging the Myth of Nonpolitical Technology

Introduction

This book of essays covers many important subjects concerning the development of political science – or political studies if you prefer, as I do. They include going back to the beginnings to analyse contributions of the London School of Economics, the Hochschule für Politik in Berlin and Columbia University in the U.S.; the transition to democracy in Germany; the contributions of such leaders as Klaus von Beyme to the globalization of the discipline; and the role of technology, specialization, team work, and political philosophy and economy to the broadening of political studies.

One has to have special talents to cover such a gamut of studies. Rainer Eisfeld has them. His beginnings in economics and winning the Faculty Dissertation Award for his thesis at Frankfurt demonstrated the obligatory interdisciplinarity and rigour required for studies of the discipline. This early promise was then molded into his position as a senior scholar by his long career at the University of Osnabrück and his leadership in the fields of pluralism and analysis of the discipline in the International Political Science Association. All of which means that he has quite a background to share with us in this his most recent collection of essays.

I have known and worked with Rainer for the past two decades. I have always been struck by two characteristics: his disciplined approached to political studies which cloaks an underlying passionate and dedicated human being.

John Trent
Chelsea, Quebec
(Canada)

Preface

This small book represents a companion volume to my 2012 collection of articles entitled *Radical Approaches to Political Science: Roads Less Traveled,* also published by Barbara Budrich. Its chapters – like those which made up the earlier work – are based on an approach to political science **informed** by a theory of participatory pluralism (my intellectual debts are to Harold J. Laski and Robert A. Dahl), and **grounded** in history (a field in which Hans Rosenberg and Norbert Elias have been my mentors). If such an approach should be frowned upon by the "mainstream" of today's political science, that is exactly the reason why part of the earlier book's title read *Roads Less Traveled.* The present title is more conventional – for the simple reason that I have been unable to come up with a sufficiently subversive one covering the book's chapters. (Readers of the earlier volume may recall that *Roads Less Traveled* derived from an inspired suggestion by my Ottawa colleague and friend Leslie Pal.)

The collection comprises nine chapters, in contrast to its predecessor's twelve. Mostly, those were also more extensive texts. My defense is that much of my research and writing of recent years has been absorbed by the "Eschenburg Controversy" – a prolonged (and often acerbic) debate revolving around the involvement, during the Nazi regime, of one of the "founding fathers" of post-1945 West German political science in the "Aryanization" of Jewish firms. (Employed by the textile industry, Theodor Eschenburg had served as cartel manager from 1933-1945.)

British academic David Childs erred when, in his obituary (*Independent*, Aug. 3, 1999), he attested Eschenburg to have "emerged from the ruins of Hitler's Reich with an unblemished record". Anne Rohstock (Tübingen) and I found documentary proof that Eschenburg had not merely participated, during 1938/39, by opinions and suggestions in the "Aryanization" – or the liquidation – of at least three Jewish companies in Berlin and Vienna. In 1941, he had virtually hounded a Jewish entrepreneur, with whom Denmark's occupation by German forces had caught up after he had already been expropriated once in Berlin and emigrated to Copenhagen by 1939. Eschenburg pushed *("ich bitte nochmals um Beschleunigung")* the Reich Foreign Trade Agency to double-check whether the company, which the Agency had earlier pronounced "Aryan", was not actually Jewish. In that case, he threatened to "cut off the firm's supply" with raw materials. Eschenburg emerged as an example of a conservative non-Nazi (*staatskonservativ*, in his own words) who, even while maintaining personal contacts with Jews, had assiduously placed himself at the service of the racist regime.[1]

When I became involved in the debate, I had, since the early 1990s, on and off addressed three pertinent questions: Collaboration (by professional elites with the Nazi regime before 1945); continuity (of functional elites after 1945); and self-exculpation (of those elites through silence or lies). In the present collection, the two concluding chapters attest to that research, focusing on Wernher von Braun, presumed "Columbus of Space", his Peenemünde team of engineers, and their involvement in the Nazi slave labor program.

For Germany's political science "mainstream", such historically grounded concerns figure, once again, no longer among salient issues. That point of view contrasts markedly with the attitude of the first two generations of West German political scientists, who perceived exploring the origins, instruments, and consequences of Nazism as a *sine qua non* of the discipline (names like Karl Dietrich Bracher, Ernst Fraenkel, Eugen Kogon, Franz L. Neumann, Kurt Sontheimer instantly spring to mind). Subsequently, those topics were relegated to the margins of an increasingly "actualist" (Klaus von Beyme) discipline. They become the nearly exclusive turf of contemporary historians – a process which has hardly proved to the advantage of political science.

Without exception, the chapters included here have benefited from the intellectual enrichment that proved such a rewarding experience during my six years' service on the International Political Science Association's Executive Committee. The same holds true, in many profound ways, for the two decades that I have now been serving, sole political scientist among committed historians, on the Board of Trustees of the Buchenwald and Mittelbau-Dora Concentration Camp Memorials.

Three chapters are first publications. The others originally appeared in countries as widely apart as Canada and Poland, the United Kingdom, the Ukraine, and Germany. Once again, I remain indebted to Barbara Budrich for agreeing to assemble these dispersed writings between two covers.

And I am deeply grateful to John Trent for the personal warmth of the introduction which he contributed to the book. John's term as IPSA Secretary General (1976-1988) is not least remembered for the 1979 World Congress in

---

1   See, most comprehensively, Rainer Eisfeld: "Theodor Eschenburg und der Raub jüdischer Vermögen 1938/39" (Dokumentation), *Vierteljahrshefte für Zeitgeschichte* 62 (2014), 603-62; Anne Rohstock: „Vom Anti-Parlamentarier zum ‚kalten Arisierer' jüdischer Unternehmen in Europa. Theodor Eschenburg in Weimarer Republik und Drittem Reich", *Vierteljahrshefte für Zeitgeschichte* 63 (2015), 33-58; Rainer Eisfeld (ed.): *Mitgemacht. Theodor Eschenburgs Beteiligung an „Arisierungen" im Nationalsozialismus*, Wiesbaden: Springer VS 2015.

Moscow and for the effort to get China into the IPSA fold. More recently, at the 2008 Montréal regional Conference and the 2009 Santiago World Congress, John Trent launched and led a debate on the relevance of political science – a debate that has continued to reverberate through the discipline and, it may safely be predicted, will not go away soon.

What Political Science May (Not) Achieve

By 2006, APSR editor Lee Sigelman (George Washington University), whose untimely death saddened the discipline three years later, saw political science as having moved, during recent decades, "in the direction of being a federation of loosely linked specialties": Sigelman argued that sub-fields and organized sections, often with their specialized journals, had been emerging as cores around which "more and more of [the discipline's] intellectual and organizational life has come to revolve". That same year, IPSA – the International Political Science Association – embarked on a "linkage" policy with regard to its Research Committees, intended to mitigate the problematic consequences of excessive specialization. Serving as IPSA's Research Committee Representative from 2006-2012, I was involved in that effort. At the end of my two terms, I tried to draw a few lessons for the discipline from recent experience in a keynote address at the joint IPSA RC 2/RC 37 Conference "Rethinking Political Development: Multifaceted Role of Elites and Transforming Leadership" (Rollins College, Florida, November 7, 2011), which subsequently was published in the IPSA Bulletin Participation.

Specialization and Teamwork:
Current Challenges to the Discipline

I

During 2011, in a process I feel privileged to have been part of, the International Political Science Association's Executive Committee agreed on the first mission statement in IPSA's history. That mission is now posted on the IPSA website. It embodies two distinct visions: one of service to the community, and a second of organizing research with an intention of assuring the high caliber of that service. To quote from the first:

> Political science...(aims) at contribut(ing) to the quality of public deliberation and decision-making...Ultimately, IPSA supports the role of political science in empowering men and women to participate more effectively in political life, whether within or beyond the states in which they live.

I am labeling that statement a "vision", as opposed to a description, because to a large extent it jars with Giovanni Sartori's 2004 contention, according to which political science – at least American-style, largely quantitative political science – "is going nowhere... Practice-wise, it is a largely useless science that does not supply knowledge for use"[1]. In a more recent, but no less skep-

---

1   Sartori, Giovanni (2004): "Where is Political Science Going?", *PS* 11, 785-786 (786).

tical assessment, Joseph Nye suggests that the discipline may be "moving in the direction of saying more and more about less and less".[2]

Such statements reflect misgivings stemming from a debate about the compartmentalization, balkanization, and fragmentation of political science that has continued to flare up. They also reflect concerns how much relevant, stimulating, important work is being done in the discipline's fields. The debate captured unexpected media attention in November 2009, when a Republican senator's motion, which would have prohibited the American National Science Foundation "from wasting federal research funding on political science projects", obtained 36 votes in the U.S. Senate.[3] While the motion, it might be argued, says more about the current Republican Party than about political science, the vote and the rationale for the motion nevertheless may serve as a caveat to the discipline. I will return to the issue in a moment.

Appropriately enough, IPSA, through its mission statement, aims at strengthening the discipline so that it may better be able to fulfil its envisioned purpose of serving democracy. Again, I quote:

> IPSA's research committees encourage the world-wide pooling of skills and resources by working both together and in conjunction with specialist sub-groups of national asassociations... Linking scholars from North and South as well as East and West, IPSA seeks to strengthen the networks that underpin a global political science community.

Some 40 years ago, at the VIII World Congress held in Munich in 1970, IPSA decided to institutionalize research activities throughout the world by setting up research committees. The immediate establishment of a large number of such committees signaled that our association had indeed responded to growing demands for sustained cooperation among political scientists. Since 2006, IPSA has been pursuing a policy of strengthening links and forging new ties among Research Committees, and between RCs and national political science associations belonging to IPSA as collective members. Efforts at teamwork across sub-fields and countries are deemed essential for creating synergies and making the most of existing specialization. Again, I will expound on these considerations shortly.

---

2   Quoted by writer Patricia Cohen in the *New York Times*, October 19, 2009 (www.nytimes. com/2009/10/20/books/20poli.html, accessed May 27, 2010).
3   Cf. http://www.senate.gov/legislative/LIS/roll_call_lists/roll_call_vote; http://coburn.senate. gov/public/index.cfm? FuseAction=RightNow, both accessed May 27, 2010.

II

Not just IPSA's Research Committees had proliferated. By 2010, 13 national political science associations had collectively generated no fewer than 216 research-oriented standing sub-groups, sections or working committees. Four national organizations alone – the British Political Studies Association, the American, German, and Russian Political Science Associations – gave rise to some 147 such groups or committees. *As befits polities and societies largely characterized by the structures and processes of 'interest-group liberalism' (Theodore J. Lowi), the specialization of – albeit loosely – organized groups has been supplementing, if not to some extent replacing, the specialization of individual scholars.*

As a matter of course, the research interests of these groups often overlap. Yet while individual members of various committees continue to collaborate, in many instances there is little or no mutual awareness of each other's projects, meetings, or publications. Problems of "turf", i. e existing priorities, incentives and responsibilities, seem to work as the chief barrier to greater cooperation between research groups. By early 2010, four years after IPSA launched its "linkage" policy, hardly one third of its 50 research committees had organized joint activities. A much smaller minority had forged links with national associations, or their sub-sections.

The discipline's compartmentalization has been tied to the emergence of "niches" where highly specialized political scientists conduct "highly particularized" research, eventually writing for "highly specialized audiences rather than... [for] a few specialists and many non-specialists".[4] John Trent, the former IPSA Secretary General, who organized our association's world congresses from 1973 to 1988, and in 2000, earlier this year set out some obvious consequences when he highlighted the discipline's "retreat from domestic public debate ... There are few 'public intellectuals' and few connections with the political class". The general result, Trent concluded, is "a sense that we are not helping citizens."[5] The same self-centered "neglect of the citizen" was attested to our discipline in a recent interview by 2009 Economics Laureate Elinor Ostrom, who will be keynote speaker at the 2012 IPSA World Congress.[6]

Soberingly enough, both Ostrom's and Trent's observations are consistent with the reasons U. S. Senator Thomas Coburn (R, OK) read into the

---

4 Sigelman, Lee (2006): "The Coevolution of American Political Science and the American Political Science Review", *APSR* 100, 463-478 (475).

5 Trent, John (2011): "Should Political Science be More Relevant? An Empirical and Critical Analysis of the Discipline", *EPS* 10, 191-209 (196/197).

6 Cf. Toonen, Theo (2010): "Resilience in Public Administration: The Work of Elinor and Vincent Ostrom from a Public Administration Perspective", *Public Administration Review* 70, 193-202 (197). – Sadly, Elinor Ostrom died a few weeks before the 2012 Madrid Congress.

record when submitting the motion which he intended to have voted into law as Coburn Amendment 2631 to the 2010 Commerce, Justice & Science Appropriation Act. As mentioned, the amendment would have barred the National Science Foundation from allocating funds to any political science project. Such funds, Coburn maintained, should rather be spent on endeavours "yield[ing] breakthroughs and discoveries that can improve the human condition."[7] The implication was obvious.

In stark contrast to such harsh assessments of the current state of the art, the APSA Task Force on Graduate Education, in its 2004 Report to the APSA Council, argued for a commitment of the discipline that would involve nothing less than *a substantial reversal of presently prevailing trends*. Its members included Kristen Monroe at Irvine, Robert Keohane at Duke, Michael Wallerstein (now sadly deceased) at Northwestern and Rogers M. Smith at Penn. The Task Force insisted that both *exploring* ways in which politics can "help resolve human difficulties", and *communicating* "to broader audiences" how the *study* of politics may aid in "achiev[ing] improved understandings of substantively important features of human life" should rank foremost among the tasks of our discipline.[8]

I have expressed largely identical opinions elsewhere:[9] We may expect to continue living in an era of globalization-induced financial and economic crises, increasing ethno-cultural pluralisation, and millenarian violence. In such an environment, both policy-makers and citizens grapple with a plethora of economic, political and cultural challenges. It is vital that political studies should address these challenges. Emphasizing broad societal participation in the shaping of public policies, the discipline should make a determined effort "to help citizens prepare themselves for various possible futures".[10] Otherwise, "perplexity, distrust, fear and intolerance" – the intolerance born of distrust and fear – may overwhelm large segments of society,[11] making them lash out against democratic principles and practices.

---

7   As in n. 3.
8   Cf. www.apsanet.org/content_2470.cfm, 3 (accessed October 5, 2011).
9   Eisfeld, Rainer (2011): "How Political Science Might Regain Relevance and Obtain an Audience: A Manifesto for the 21st Century", *EPS* 10, 220-225. See also id. (2011): "Towards Creating a Discipline With a 'Regional Stamp': Central-East European Political Science and Ethno-Cultural Diversity", *Lithuanian Foreign Policy Review*, No. 25, 121-129. Both articles have been reprinted in Eisfeld, Rainer (2012): *Radical Approaches to Political Science: Roads Less Traveled*, Opladen/Berlin/Toronto, 13-19.
10 Hankiss, Elemér (2002): "Brilliant Ideas or Brilliant Errors? Twelve Years of Social Science Research in Eastern Europe", in: Max Kaase/Vera Sparschuh (eds.): *Three Social Science Disciplines in Central and Eastern Europe*, Berlin/Budapest, 17-24 (22).
11 Ibid. (20).

17

III

Where to begin, and how to involve IPSA's research committees? An answer might be: in the spirit of Montréal. IPSA's 2008 Montréal intermediate conference, titled "Political Science in the World: New Theoretical and Regional Perspectives", systematically brought together RCs and national associations for the first time in the history of IPSA. Some 150 delegates from over 30 countries represented 27 research committees and 23 national associations. The Montréal event was followed by a 2010 Luxembourg mid-term conference on models of European governance, co-sponsored by the Luxembourg Political Science Association, and in 2011 by a joint IPSA-ECPR event – another first – hosted by the Brazilian Political Science Association. Its thematic focus was the continued relevance of the international North-South divide.

These conferences stood out by virtue of their emphasis on *cross-field studies transcending the domains of our discipline's traditional sub-fields. Cutting across time-honoured boundaries, engaging salient issue areas in terms of over-arching approaches and themes, it is such cross-field research which may be expected to stimulate the discipline's return to an agenda marked by a broader intellectual scope, more innovative content, and greater public relevance.* It should be noted that cross-field studies and teaching are presently emphasized by political science departments at, e.g., the New School for Social Research, the University of Massachusetts Amherst, and the University of Colorado at Boulder.

The Montréal Conference certainly pointed the way toward the pursuit of research initiatives patterned after that formula, and the Luxembourg and Sao Paulo follow-up events provided further inspiration. But the crucial role falls to IPSA's research committees. They must keep the ball rolling. And at that point, the significance of the present conference on the multi-faceted roles of elites and transforming leadership in political development, hosted by RCs 37 and 2, comes into play.

What topic could be more relevant, in the sense of addressing one or more of today's vexing political issues, than such a focus on the role of players, both elites and mass movements, in the Arab uprisings around the Mediterranean and in the volatile countries of East and South-East Asia? And what could make more sense, for the purposes of such an inquiry, than pooling the intellectual resources of IPSA's research groups on the recruitment and performance of political elites and on innovative, cross-cultural approaches to political development?

A joint effort devoted to salient issues has ensued, and the following questions have been raised: From which families, clans or parties might new elites in these regions emerge? Can we expect them to be more accountable, less corrupt, more willing to acknowledge the rights of women and minorities? What chances do the mass movements which have recently carried the day, have of attaining their objectives – quality of life, social justice, in the last instance human dignity? Will the West respond more sensibly than in the past, finally acknowledging these countries as developing polities and societies in their own right, rather than automatically invoking considerations of "security", "strategic importance", and access to natural resources? Both *formally*, with experts participating from two research committees and a dozen countries, and *substantively*, with regard to the issues being explored, this meeting offers the kind of perspective on the study of politics which is essential to the progress of our discipline.

I should like to invoke one more example of the kind of efforts that I have in mind, to which IPSA's research committees can make a crucial contribution. In June, 2010, the Russian Political Science Association, the non-governmental Saint Petersburg Center for Humanities and Political Studies, and the International Political Science Association's Research Committee on Politics and Ethnicity jointly organized a conference on "Ethno-Cultural Diversity and the Problem of Tolerance" in St. Petersburg. Several of the major presentations focused on a feature central to current societies, which the migration component of globalisation may be safely predicted to produce on an increasing scale: the recourse to ethnicity as a source of social identification and identity – not just for these societies' minorities, but also for their *majorities*.

How much heterogeneity will these majorities accept? How may cultural narratives be advanced, which promote mutual "recognition" and tolerance, rather than separation and conflict? Should political science attempt to develop concepts replacing the idea of a single identity by the notion of "a set of identities" that would allow the individual "to participate in various [cultural] communities"?[12]

Once again, it is results of such collaborative efforts from which "lay inquiries" by citizens and policy-makers alike might benefit.[13] If sessions at world political sciences congresses (henceforth held every two years) should succeed in communicating that same impression to wider audiences, we will be taking another step toward fulfilling IPSA's mission.

---

12 Kuznetsov, Anatoliy (2010): "Political Science Before a Challenge of Ethno-Cultural Pluralism", in: *Ethno-Cultural Diversity and the Problem of Pluralism in a Globalizing World*, Conference Proceedings, St. Peters-burg, 96-110 (96).

13 Cf. Lindblom, Charles E. (1990): Inquiry and Change. *The Troubled Attempt to Understand and Shape Society*, New Haven/London, 216/217, 257/1258. For a ray of hope in present-day German political science, see the brief piece by Bommarius, Christian (2011): "Die Rache der Feuilletonisten. Die Politologie sucht endlich das offene Gespräch", *Frankfurter Rundschau*, 67, No. 230 (October 4, 2011), 10.

The science of politics has been portrayed as unavoidably imbued by democratic ideals, its development tied to the evolution of a democratic polity: An inherently "moral" discipline according to Samuel Huntington ("Political Science and Political Reform", American Political Science Review, 1988), bound to contribute, at the very least "in small ways", to "the emergence and stabilization of democracy". Such a narrative provides a powerful image, because it adds ethical legitimacy to the field. Even before Huntington's dictum, not just the post-1945, but also the pre-1933 variety of German political science was thus embellished, presented as a "thoroughly republican-democratic enterprise" whose scholars were supposed to have uniformly rejected any cooperation with the Nazis. Was this true? Or was it merely a convenient myth which persisted well into the 1980s? And how did political science respond to the situation Germany found itself in by 1945? Or to post-1989 developments? The following chapter appeared in 2012 as part of a collected volume edited by Anatoliy Kruglashov of the Chernivtsi (Ukraine) National University's Department of Political Science and Public Administration.

Political Science and Transition to Democracy: The German Experience

I

How does an academic discipline, *any* academic discipline, evolve? What association exists between developments in higher education and broader changes, social as well as political?

Political science provides *the* outstanding example of a field whose evolution was shaped, to a very considerable degree, by contextual factors – such as a particular country's system of government, its predominant patterns of ideological orientation and of political behavior. And if we look around for a country where drastic changes in these areas have occurred not once or twice, but repeatedly in the course of the 20th century, Germany emerges as a surefire candidate.

Was political science, as has been claimed, "inherently democratic" and consequently doomed for twelve years, after the Nazis had come to power? Might not authoritarian-totalitarian regimes, such as Nazi Germany, hold attractions for scholars in the social no less than in the engineering and natural sciences? Why should only a physicist like Werner Heisenberg, have entered into what is usually referred to as "a Faustian pact" with National Socialism (Walker 1995: 269)? Why should only a missile engineer, like Wernher von

Braun, later acclaimed as "the free world's leading authority on space travel", have allowed himself to become implicated in the infamous Nazi slave labor program, so that his V-2 rocket might be mass-produced by concentration camp inmates (see Neufeld 1995; Eisfeld 1996b)?

Material support and official prestige certainly figure among possible rewards. However, reasons for a lack of immunity against anti-democratic temptations may also prove to be more deep-seated.

Arnold Bergstraesser, who held the chair of Political Science (or, as the German metaphor would have it, *Staatswissenschaft*) and Foreign Studies at the University of Heidelberg, professed in late 1933 that he had "felt for many years that nothing but dictatorship would restore order and confidence in Germany" (Bergstraesser 1934: 44). Adolf Grabowsky and Richard Schmidt, co-editors of the *Zeitschrift für Politik* ('Journal of Politics'), concurred with Bergstraesser: A "national awakening, even if it led to more oppression", was to be "preferred over crippling passivity", "an injustice over disarray" (Grabowsky 1932: 370; Schmidt 1933: 91).

More often than not, dictatorships will compel *those* scholars to leave their home country who share a commitment to liberty and human dignity, equal rights and opportunities, government by majority rule. The Nazi regime added racist reasons to the grounds for expelling large numbers of intellectuals. Yet, the Nazis also had use for the social sciences, and in the case of those who chose to remain and to collaborate, distinctions became blurred between scholars and ideologues.

These facts are bound to raise some rather sobering questions about the seductive chances offered by totalitarian/authoritarian regimes. They suggest reflection not merely on the significance of opposition and exile for the survival and revival of political science, but also on the extent and the reasons for not a few political scientists' susceptibility to authoritarian programs.

This article will consequently focus on five issue areas:

To what extent, and why, had political scientists proved amenable to collaboration with the Nazis, in contrast to those who fled into exile? How had the so-called Third Reich proceeded to adapt the discipline to its purposes? When the curtain came down in 1945, what happened to the scholars who had served as compliant tools of the regime's politics? Who were the political and academic players bent on resurrecting the discipline in a democratized West Germany? Finally, what did these players expect from political science, which major obstacles were they facing, to what extent did they succeed in their vision?

II

Discounting, for the purposes of this brief analysis, an earlier tradition of philosophical-historical *Staatslehre* (see Bleek 2001: ch. 4), beginnings of political science emerged in Germany after World War I, with a foothold in a few universities (such as Hamburg, Heidelberg, or Leipzig), but mainly extramurally, at the German Institute of Politics (*Deutsche Hochschule für Politik*) located in Berlin. Aimed at providing adult political education by offering evening classes, the Institute was established in 1920 as a privately run facility, following World War I and the revolution which had resulted in Germany's first parliamentary-democratic polity, usually referred to as the Weimar Republic (after the city where a constituent assembly had drafted the new constitution). The necessary funds were provided, first and foremost, by the new governments of Germany and of the state of Prussia, supplemented by grants from a few liberal industrialists such as Bosch or Siemens. After 1926/27, further financial support came from the Rockefeller Foundation and the Carnegie Endowment for International Peace (see Korenblat 1978: 92 ss., 205 ss.).

As the Institute's shared value, its leadership proclaimed a stance above political parties, an appeal for non-partisan consensus and independence. So why would the Institute's faculty differ markedly in their degree of immunity to the antidemocratic temptation held forth by the Nazis?

The individuals who set up and governed the Institute – prominent among them liberal political journalists Ernst Jäckh and Theodor Heuss, who would become West Germany's first president after 1945 – held several firmly established convictions. The first of these was that widespread "unpolitical" attitudes and patterns of behavior in German society had favored both the emergence of the authoritarian state in 1871 and its defeat by 1918. Therefore, the German people needed to be educated politically, a task not exactly favored by the constraints of the country's traditional system of higher education. A second shared belief was that, in a parliamentary democracy, the selection and training of capable political leaders constituted *the* major problem. Such over-emphasis on leadership did not least derive from Germany's authoritarian past, and before long, the leadership ideal would be tied to what might be termed "great-man doctrines", favoring an anti-parliamentary and antidemocratic backlash (see Struve 1973: 9; Faulenbach 1980: 310).

The almost metaphysical significance which leadership came to acquire during the 1920s had a lot to do with a third opinion firmly held by large segments of the population and certainly by an overwhelming majority among the Weimar Republic's prominent political and academic figures: That the peace treaty concluding World War I had been unjust and needed to be revised. Defeat in the war had come as a shock to Germany, and a pronounced revisionism rejecting the peace settlement, bent on re-establishing the country's pre-war position of power, came to pervade Weimar Germany's society during the nineteen twenties (see Salewski 1980: passim). In theory as in practice, it reinforced a functional, instrumentalist approach to both domestic and foreign policy. If democratic government, if cooperation with the League of Nations – forerunner to today's United Nations – proved unable to achieve revision, both might be expendable.

On top of that, a growing element among the Berlin Institute's faculty – self-styled "conservative revolutionaries", as they called themselves – subscribed to a radicalized, nationalist version of revisionism, unwilling, as they proclaimed, "to let the fatherland perish by the hands of inadequate leaders and external enemies" (Spahn 1922: 3). The Institute split along conceptual lines. On the one hand, scholars of democratic persuasion – mostly Social Democrats according to party affiliation – would teach an approach to domestic and foreign politics focusing on equality and social justice, on peaceful conflict settlement, an abandonment of territorial demands and renunciation of hegemony. They either lost their positions in 1933, or were forced into exile. After 1945, these were the individuals who would come to play a decisive part in the re-establishment of the Berlin Institute.

On the other hand, the Institute's positions and publications were open to those intransigent nationalist enemies of the Weimar Republic, whose approach centered on four basic tenets: A "homogeneous" nation, rooted in "blood and soil", distinct from "atomistic" and "divisive"modern society; a corporatist, supposedly "organic" state, replacing "mechanistic" Western parliamentarism; a belief in authoritarian political leadership, as opposed to democratic "levelling"; finally, the perspective of renewed German hegemony in central Europe as a "continuing German mission". This approach amounted to *politicized*, rather than political science. Inevitably, it paved the way for the Nazi doctrine that *no* science could escape being political science – in the sense that it had to serve purposes laid down by political, i. e. Nazi, authorities (see Eisfeld 1991: 44).

Moreover, the process of "imposing conformity" (*Gleichschaltung*) on the discipline after 1933 came to be effectively assisted by those sometime "republicans by force of reason" (*Vernunftrepublikaner*) like Bergstraesser, Schmidt and Grabowsky to whom the article referred at the outset, and whose resentful discontent lent itself to political irresponsibility. Bergstraesser contributed to academic Nazification by replacing scholarly with political performance criteria, approving doctoral theses which were mere tracts, but resulted in doctorates that would serve as cornerstones for many a subsequent career (see Eisfeld 1996a: 46/47). On the basis of pseudo-scholarly reasoning, Schmidt came to justify the emasculation of political science in Nazi Germany, arguing that "the focus and method of political science" should be "thoroughly recast", leaving only Foreign Studies – *Auslandskunde* – in place (Schmidt 1938: 12, 14/15).

III

That perspective perfectly suited the Nazi regime which was interested in re-cruiting internationally knowledgeable personnel. What the Nazis demanded from the discipline for their purposes amounted, in their own jargon, to "po-litical topography" – exploring, for instance, the American conception of neutrality, the role of German minorities in Canada, or French armament pol-icies. However, the performance of the Berlin Institute, which had been run by the Propaganda Ministry since 1933, proved increasingly unimpressive. Because it could not confer a university degree, it did not attract qualified students.

By the late 1930s, another player entered the debate on the Institute's fu-ture: Heinrich Himmler, powerful head of the SS, the Nazi Party's self-styled elite corps. For its Security Service, the SS had recruited a number of aca-demically educated Nazis – men who were resolved to transform ideological myths into "bureaucratically applicable lucidity" (Aronson 1967: 276). The elitist SS self-image additionally spurred a determined academic policy which the SS started to pursue by 1938/39 and which was made easier by the considerable number of members which the SS had attracted among the Edu-cation Ministry's senior civil servants (see Heiber 1966: 124; Kater 1974: 132).

In 1940, a new Department of Foreign Studies was established at the University of Berlin, integrating the Berlin Institute. The individual put in charge as permanent dean was Franz Alfred Six, who had obtained doctoral and postdoctoral qualifications by submitting mere pamphlets at the Univer-sity of Heidelberg during the early 1930s, and had more recently been ap-pointed both associate professor of journalism and head of the Security Ser-vice division on "Enemy Investigation". The department offered a foreign studies degree after 6 semesters. Dossiers of students who either professed an interest in intelligence work or seemed "suitable", were regularly passed on to the Security Service. The propagandist rhetoric of its faculty was directed toward the promise of a European "New Order" which German hegemony would build throughout the occupied continent. To the final hour of the Nazi regime, Foreign Studies remained a politically manipulated discipline.

The department was immediately dissolved, after Germany had been conquered by the Allies. Six, who had terminated his career as SS-Brigade-führer, equivalent in rank to a Major General, was sentenced to twenty years imprisonment by an American Military Tribunal for his two months' partici-pation in one of the mobile SS extermination units which had started the sys-tematic massacres of Jews in occupied Soviet Russia. Like many other con-victed war criminals, he was released in 1952, subsequent to a shift in Amer-ican policy triggered by the Cold War. He became a marketing expert and basically faded from the scene (see Eisfeld 1996a: 49/50; Hachmeister 1998: chs. VIII/IX).

IV

Several other rapid academic careers, however, which had been started by the establishment of the Foreign Studies Department, would be continued after the war – not in political science, but in international and public law, in sociology, in history (see 9, p. 50). These individuals' reinstatement did not meet with any resistance on campuses where an overwhelming majority of academics clung to the belief that Germany's universities had survived the Nazi regime as the "standard bearers of an old and basically sound tradition" (Heimpel 1956: 7). Small wonder that university rectors after 1945 responded with reserve, distrust, even scorn to the idea that the introduction of social studies curricula might contribute to a renewal of Germany's traditional education system (see Eisfeld 1988: 26).

Political science owed its eventual establishment as an academic discipline to a coalition of exiled scholars, American occupation officers, and German politicians – mostly Social Democrats, with a few Christian Democrats added. In a 1947 memorandum to the American Military Government, Hajo Holborn was the first to recommend the resurrection of the Berlin Institute. Holborn, who had taught there before emigrating and had again emerged as a brilliant political historian at Yale University, suggested that the Institute should return to its extramural status, so that admission to its courses might be handled more liberally, reaching out to people outside the normal academic strata (see Lange-Quassowski 1979: 227, 301 n. 724).

In pressing for the Institute's re-establishment, Holborn was joined by Otto Suhr, who had also counted among its pre-1933 instructors, was now serving as social-democratic chair of West Berlin's City Council, and would subsequently rise to the position of Lord Mayor. He became the Institute's first director, when it was re-opened by late 1949. Suhr's thinking, in common with other leading Social Democrats, revolved around the problem how future generations might be politically educated so as to prevent another destruction of democracy. In their efforts, they met with those by American occupation officers who aimed at re-educating the German people toward the acceptance of democratic values by placing increased emphasis on social studies. When the military government retreated from more ambitious plans for reorganizing German education along American lines, political science seemed to provide an input which might at least serve to make students more aware of social and political realities *and* responsibilities.

The Office of U.S. Military Government (OMGUS) and subsequently the American High Commissioner in Germany (HICOG), who took over from OMGUS after the Federal Republic of Germany had been founded in 1949, sponsored several conferences on political science in cooperation with German state governments, particularly their Departments of Education. (Already earlier, a few isolated political science chairs had been established by these same governments, against delaying tactics pursued by the universities.) In his opening address, the Minister of Education of the state of Hesse which hosted the first such conference emphasized that a discipline was needed which proceeded from a "science of national citizenship" to a "science of world citizenship". He stressed that political science would have to convey the evils of nationalism and racial hatred, the reprehensibleness of war as a means of politics, and the importance of mutual understanding in foreign relations (see *Die politischen Wissenschaften* 1949: 8, 11) – tasks that have remained nothing less than topical.

Three such conferences, held in 1949 and 1950, were attended by exiled and other untainted German scholars, by politicians and civil servants. With overwhelming majorities, the participants argued in favor of incorporating the discipline into academic curricula. In 1954, the Committee of West German University Presidents finally gave its blessings to the establishment of a sizable number of political science chairs. A second surge in chairs followed after a spate of neo-Nazi and antisemitic graffiti swept through German cities in late 1959 and early 1960. It turned out that most of these acts had been committed by youths bent on desecrating Jewish cemeteries and synagogues. The Conference of States' Education Ministers reacted by finally pushing political education with greater vigor. Political science students might henceforth pursue a teaching career in the new school subject of civic studies – a substantial incentive for student enrolment and for the enlargement of political science departments.

Regarding the discipline's dominant paradigm during the first two decades of West Germany's existence, both the experience of American exile and the Cold War had worked as formative influences. The paradigm focused on the institutions and decision-making processes of parliamentary democracies, with a special emphasis on political parties and interest groups, and on the distinction of Western political pluralism from "totalitarian rule", both of the Nazi and of the Communist variety. Experience of the Nazi reign of terror and of life-saving emigration, plus the Cold War confrontation in divided Germany, led to a moral identification of the formerly exiled scholars with the United States as the exponent of Western democracy. Political science in West Germany, during the first two decades after the country's transition to democracy, was a highly normative discipline, suited for political education, but largely devoid of empirical research and methodological reflection.

Did that discipline contribute in any way to West Germany's democratization? Certainly insofar, as any renewed option for alleged German distinctiveness, for a "peculiar" German political course, remained excluded. No ideology emerged again that aimed at setting Germany apart from the values of 1688, 1776 and 1789 – from the tenets of parliamentary democracy and human rights, as they had been translated into practice by a succession of revolutions in England, America and France. The efforts of political scientists thus paralleled the policy of West German governments of integrating the country into the Western alliance.

V

Again for two decades, the introduction of political science as an academic discipline remained the sole modification imprinted on the traditional German university structure by a unique coalition of victorious Allies, exiled scholars and German politicians. That would change with the advent of the students-based political movement of radical dissent in the late 1960s. Challenging ossified academic hierarchies, its proponents pushed for more educational, political, industrial democracy. The militants, and not a few liberal sympathizers, argued in favor of rearranging social science research priorities "in the light of a better understanding of own value assumptions", including the construction of political alternatives (Eastern 1969: 1058/1059).

In the West German case, the erstwhile political science paradigm had already started to dissolve through reception of the behavioralist and systems theory approaches of American political science. It became further undermined as the accession to government of a Grand Coalition – the first in West Germany – in 1966 was followed by the passing of emergency powers legislation, and as the Vietnam War suffocated Lyndon Johnson's attempts at deepening and widening the reforms achieved by Roosevelt's New Deal. Both processes fueled the protest movement.

However, the ensuing fragmentation of political science was, at the time, overrated. What, instead, had emerged in West Germany by the early 1980s was the normal picture of a considerably diversified, but firmly entrenched academic discipline. Normative orientation was on the retreat, replaced by any number of specialized policy studies based on empirical research.

The manifold problems resulting from German reunification did not change that picture. During the early 1990s, Germany started to come under the pyramiding strains of reunification-induced financial burdens, mass unemployment, and increased refugee influx from Third World countries. Resulting from economic anxieties, ideological disorientation and perplexed insecurity, blatantly social-Darwinist and racist attitudes have continued to fuel

27

attacks on asylum applicants and other foreigners, on homeless and on handicapped people, particularly in what used to be the German Democratic Republic. A racist adolescent sub-culture has emerged in Germany's new states. Lacking an organizational nucleus, it consists of a network of small groups defining themselves in terms of a militant "racial avant-garde" (see Bergmann/Erb 1994: 27, Wagner 1998: 44 ss.).

Yet no analogy to the post-1960 response of states' education ministers to neo-Nazi activities has materialized. Neither have any vigorous professional initiatives been in evidence which might be compared to the post-1945 activities, when political science aspired to be an innovative force in education. In the unification process, West Germany acted as the hegemonial partner vis-a-vis the smaller, economically weaker Eastern population. German political science has tended to mirror that situation. Just as no new constitution, which might more accurately have reflected the values of a united Germany, emerged from a broad popular debate, no reflection of the "state of the art" has occurred in the discipline.

At the heart of politics – including democratic politics – are issues of power and authority, of participation and of control over agenda-setting. These issues no longer figure at the center of the discipline's attention. Rather, political science – the earlier observation bears repeating – has been dissolving into the discussion of a plethora of fragmented issues. As a union of determined specialists, it offers no disciplinary profile and no normative "vision". That is the sobering result, on which the discipline's present observer must conclude.

References

Aronson, Shlomo (1967): *Heydrich und die Anfänge des SD und der Gestapo* (1931-1935), Diss. Berlin

Bergmann, Werner/Erb, Rainer (1994): „Eine soziale Bewegung von rechts?", *Neue Soziale Bewegungen*, No. 2, 83-88

Bergstraesser, Arnold (1934): "The Economic Policy of the German Government", *International Affairs*, Vol. 13, 26-46

Bleek, Wilhelm (2001): *Geschichte der Politikwissenschaft in Deutschland*, Munich: C. H. Beck

Die politischen Wissenschaften an den deutschen Universitäten und Hochschulen. Protokoll der Konferenz von Waldleiningen 1949, Wiesbaden: Hessisches Ministerium für Erziehung und Volksbildung

Easton, David (1969): "The New Revolution in Political Science", *American Political Science Review*, Vol. 68, 1051-1062

Eisfeld, Rainer (1988): "Exile and Return: Political Science in the Context of (West-) German University Development from Weimar to Bonn", *History of Higher Education Annual*, Vol. 8, 9-43

Eisfeld, Rainer (1991): *Ausgebürgert und doch angebräunt. Deutsche Politikwissenschaft 1920-1945*, Baden-Baden: Nomos

Eisfeld, Rainer (1996a): "German Political Science at the Crossroads: The Ambivalent Response to the 1933 Nazi Seizure of Power", in: id./Michael Th. Greven/Hans Karl Rupp: *Political Science and Regime Change in 20th Century Germany*, New York: Nova, 17-53

Eisfeld, Rainer (1996b): *Mondsüchtig. Wernher von Braun und die Geburt der Raumfahrt aus dem Geist der Barbarei*, Rowohlt: Reinbek

Faulenbach, Bernd (1980): *Ideologie des deutschen Weges*, Munich

Grabowsky, Adolf (1932): „Vorbemerkung" zu Berkes, Theodor: „Bataille um Südosteuropa", *Zeitschrift für Politik*, Vol. 21, 369-371

Hachmeister, Lutz (1998): *Der Gegnerforscher. Die Karriere des SS-Führers Franz Alfred Six*, Munich: C. H. Beck

Heiber, Helmut (1966): *Walter Frank und sein Reichsinstitut für Geschichte des neuen Deutschlands*, Stuttgart

Heimpel, Hermann (1956): *Probleme und Problematik der Hochschulreform*, Göttingen

Huntington, Samuel P. (1988): "One Soul at a Time: Political Science and Political Reform", *American Political Science Review*, Vol. 82, 3-10

Kater, Michael H. (1974): *Das „Ahnenerbe" der SS 1935-1945*, Stuttgart

Korenblat, Steven (1978): *The Deutsche Hochschule für Politik. Public Affairs Institute for a New Germany*, Diss. Chicago

Lange-Quassowski, Jutta (1979): *Neuordnung oder Restauration?*, Opladen

Neufeld, Michael J. (1995): *The Rocket and the Reich*, New York/London: Free Press

Salewski, Michael (1980): „Das Weimarer Revisionssyndrom", *Aus Politik und Zeitgeschichte*, B 2/80 (1/12/1980), 14-25

Schmidt, Richard (1933): „Der politische Lehrgehalt in Goethes Lebenswerk", *Zeitschrift für Politik*, Vol. 22, 73-91

Schmidt, Richard (1938): *Grundriss der Allgemeinen Staatslehre oder Politik*, Stuttgart

Spahn, Martin (1922/23): „Vorspann", in: Politisches Kolleg, Hochschule für nationale Politik, *Vorlesungsverzeichnis 1922/23*, Berlin, 3

Struve, Walter (1973): *Elites Against Democracy. Leadership Ideals in Bourgeois Political Thought in Germany, 1890-1933*, Princeton

Wagner, Bernd (1998): *Rechtsextremismus und kulturelle Subversion in den neuen Ländern*, Berlin: Zentrum demokratische Kultur

Walker, Mark (1995): *Nazi Science. Myth, Truth, and the German Atomic Bomb*, New York: Plenum Press

Standing on the Shoulders of Giants

Hannah Arendt – "German thinker, Jewish emigré, American intellectual" (Otto Kallscheuer): During recent years, the work of Arendt, who was forced into exile by the Nazis in 1933, has enjoyed a spectacular renaissance. Margarethe von Trotta's highly acclaimed 2012 biographical film introduced her to a larger audience. Seyla Benhabib rightly characterized Hannah Arendt as a "brilliant and controversial political thinker – the first to conceive the phenomenon of totalitarianism as an entirely new form of power in human history". What were Arendt's criteria? Where did her approach to total rule fundamentally differ from that of another renowned political theorist, Carl Joachim Friedrich? The following chapter is the text of a talk which I gave in 2014 at a Conference on "Conceptual Contestation and Political Change", held by the University of Zagreb's Faculty of Political Science in Memoriam of Professor Ivan Prpic. The conference had been planned in his honor. Sadly, he died just a few days earlier.

> *"For the love of a tree*
> *she went out on a limb.*
> *For the love of the sea,*
> *she rocked the boat.*
> *For the love of the earth,*
> *she dug deeper…*
> *And the world was richer for her."*
> *(Charlotte Tall Mountain:*
> *"For Love of the World", 1999)*

> Elisabeth Young-Bruehl:
> *Hannah Arendt. For Love of the World*
> (A Biography, 2002)

The "Three Pillars of Hell": Hannah Arendt's Concept of Total Rule – Sources, Merits, Limits

I

After World War II, the dichotomy of "totalitarianism" and "democracy" quickly became central to Western political thinking. On the other hand, "totalitarian" and "totalitarianism" were and have remained contested terms to this day. Both notions continue to be the subject of controversial discussion by scholars and by politicians.

The concepts' early "career" was a Cold War career. During that period, they figured prominently both in academe and in politics as routinely invoked counterparts to democracy und pluralism. An observation made about pluralism by American scholar Theodore Lowi in 1967 applies as well to totalitarianism: The concept rapidly developed into a "public philosophy" routinely used by Western elites both as guideline and justification of their policies (Lowi 1967: 5 ss.).

Political scientists on the other side of the Atlantic echoed Lowi's dictum. In a 1969 essay, German scholar Gert Schäfer argued that "the 'Western' societies' political self-reflection had, to a considerable extent, found expression in the dichotomy of democracy and totalitarianism" (Schäfer 1969: 105). The author considered it obvious that the concept refused to take into account substantial differences which, on closer inspection, distinguished Nazism from Stalinism. On the whole, the concept was assessed as „scholarly inadequate" (ibid.: 108).

Two years later, German comparativist Martin Jänicke presented a monographic study on "totalitarian rule", significantly subtitled "Anatomy of a Political Concept". Jänicke set out to investigate what he termed the "utter confusion" of the concept's scholarly and political purposes. The conclusion at which he arrived read: "The notion of total rule abounds in ambiguities and inconsistencies. In case no minimal research consensus should be attainable regarding its specification and consequently the reduction of its political uses, it may confidently be abandoned and be replaced by other, less problematic terms" (Jänicke 1971: 250).

Both authors focused their description and critique on Carl Joachim Friedrich's study *Totalitarian Dictatorship* as the "most comprehensive", "most representative" approach of its kind (Jänicke 1971: 10). Three decades later, Friedrich's concept was still ranked as *the* "classical" theory of totalitarian rule (Lietzmann 1999: 16, 119 ss). That judgment could easily be attributed to Friedrich's famous – some might say notorious – six defining criteria (guiding ideology, single party regime, planned economy, system of terror, weapons and mass communication monopolies), because they suggested rigor of comparison, an "evolved" level of theory building. Yet, these very "characteristics" were drawing attention – the longer, the more – to the fact how limited structural identities between the national-socialist and the Stalinist systems actually were. Moreover, the partial transformation of Communist regimes in the post-Stalinist period prompted Friedrich – und not just Friedrich alone – to reinterpret his indicators in a way that has been castigated as "manipulation" (Jänicke 1971: 240 ss., 243 ss.).

A conclusion drawn in 1995 consequently remains valid: Carl Joachim Friedrich's and similar constructs are "ideal types insufficiently grounded in reality" which, because of their "weaknesses" and "blind spots", lack "analytical and empirical viability" (Schmalz-Bruns 1995: 127, 135).

Both studies from which I quoted earlier conceded much less space to Hannah Arendt's *Elements and Origins of Total Rule* – the title which Arendt chose for the German edition of her *Origins of Totalitarianism* – than to Friedrich's "more evolved" approach. Jänicke criticized Arendt sharply for having "abandoned the empirical, realistic analysis" of Nazism. According to Jänicke, the "analogies between National Socialism and communism" asserted by Arendt were "more often than not just highlighted for illustrative purposes" (Jänicke 1971: 84).

Schäfer demonstrated that, for Arendt, the historically unprecedented character of totalitarian rule consisted in the "alliance of permanent terror und ideological rigor", involving the inhumanly rigid execution of supposedly objective, either *natural* or *historical*, "laws". In the process, totalitarianism abolished the "fences of *human* laws" which, by hedging in spaces for political activity, had protected freedom "as a living political reality" (Arendt 1979: 466). On that issue, but also with regard to the formlessness of totalitarian rule noted by Arendt, Schäfer identified core themes linking Arendt's analysis to that which Franz Leopold Neumann, another exiled political scientist, had presented in his work *Behemoth. The Structure and Practice of National Socialism.* (Schäfer 1969: 127 ss., 130 ss.). Arendt's concern, as Schäfer made clear, had been to explore "that extreme decay of the realm of politics" which she labeled total domination, and to demonstrate the utter impossibility of politics in the sense of associated human activity in the public sphere under such rule (id. 1993: 28).

II

Hannah Arendt's concept of total rule evolved by several stages, which have meanwhile been reconstructed. Her train of thought was started in 1943 by the first, at the time hardly believable, then ever more unsettling reports ("It was as though the abyss had opened") on the Nazis' implementation of the so-called "final solution of the Jewish question". When Arendt, by late 1944/early 1945, had completed the first draft of her book, she wished to call its three parts "Antisemitism – Imperialism – Racism (or Racial Imperialism)". The term "Racial Imperialism" had been coined by Franz Leopold Neumann in his *Behemoth* (cf. Neumann [3]1966: 184 ss.), the seminal study mentioned a moment ago. Arendt's entire work was to be entitled either "The Elements of Shame" oder "The Three Pillars of Hell". The first two parts focusing on anti-Semitism and imperialism were based on articles which Arendt had already published. According to her original plans – and up to 1946 –, the third part would have exclusively dealt with Nazism (Young-Bruehl 2002: 184/185, 200, 203; Tsao 2003: 58/58).

The sections on antisemitism and imperialism were largely completed, when the perusal of several reports written by surviving concentration camp inmates caused Arendt to change her plans (Young-Bruehl 2002: 204). Among these, as indicated by the footnotes in her book, were Eugen Kogon's *SS-Staat* (1946), later brought out in the United States under the title *The Theory and Practice of Hell*; the two works *L'Univers concentrationnaire* (1946) and *Les Jours de notre mort* (1947) by French resistance fighter David Rousset; finally, an anonymously published description of the post-1939 mass deportations from Soviet-occupied Eastern Poland to Russian camps. Entitled *The Dark Side of the Moon* (1947), the book had been authored by Zoë Zajdlerova, a Pole's Irish wife who had managed to escape the deportations, from which her husband never re-emerged. In his Preface, T. S. Eliot wrote that National Socialism and Soviet Communism equally "destroy(ed)... one pattern of life" and sought to "impos(e)" on Europe "another pattern" ("Inventories of Grief" 1948: 137). In the fall of 1947, Arendt informed German philosopher Karl Jaspers that she would have to rewrite the third part, because "the real essential things, particularly with regard to Russia, [were] just now [be]coming clear" to her (Tsao 2003: 61/62, n. 5).

Reading the survivors' memoirs, Arendt concluded that the concentration camps were the "essential", the "distinguish[ing]" feature of total rule (Young-Bruehl 2002: 204). Because they served "as the laboratories in which the fundamental belief of totalitarianism that everything is possible is being verified" (Arendt 1979: 437), they supplied to totalitarian power its "true central institution" (ibid.: 438).

If the camps constitute "the most consequential institution of totalitarian rule", the secret police emerges as the system's "power nucleus" (Arendt 1979: 420, 441). SS and NKVD are entrusted by the Leader with realizing, through terror, the "totalitarian fiction", consisting in either the presumed classless society or the racist *Volksgemeinschaft* (ibid.: 421/422). Of the state, there remains but the "outward façade" (ibid.: 420). Insisting that "what strikes the observer of the totalitarian state is certainly not its monolithic structure", Arendt dismissed "the common misconception" of total rule as "tyranny" or "despotism" (ibid.: 395, 421). Painting a picture that did not deny the debt it owed to Franz Neumann's *Behemoth*, she portrayed – once again, more concisely for the Nazi than for the Stalinist regime – the "multiplication of agencies" resulting in the body politic's "planned shapelessness" (ibid.: 401, 402).

Arendt's 1953 essay "Ideology and Terror: A Novel Form of Government" provided the eventual cornerstone of her argument. In her contribution to *Offener Horizont* [Open Horizons], a commemorative publication in honor of Karl Jaspers, she formulated her thoughts about the inhuman "lawfulness" of totalitarian regimes based on assumed "law(s) of History or law(s) of Nature", to be executed on mankind (ibid.: 462). These considerations were carried over by Arendt two years later into the new concluding chapter of the *Origins'* first German, in 1958 of the revised English edition. Terror remains the "essence" of totalitarian rule (ibid.: 466). Yet it does not simply serve domination for domination's sake: While the *ideologically* stipulated processes of Nature or History are "let loose" on men, terror forces the subjects together by a "band of iron", irrevocably eradicating their capacity to act freely, meaning *politically* (ibid.: 465, 468).

By 1966, Arendt would amend her text one last time (Ludz 2003: 85 ss.). After prolonged uncertainties about the "authenticity" of Soviet "detotalitarization" (Arendt 1991: XXV), she added a new Preface to Part III, in which she limited the period of total rule in the Soviet Union to the years 1928 – 1953 (Arendt 1991: XXXVII):

> The people of the Soviet Union have emerged from the nightmare of totalitarian rule to the manifold hardships, dangers, and injustices of one-party dictatorship… This modern form of tyranny offers none of the guarantees of constitutional government, and … the country therefore can relapse into totalitarianism between one day and another without major upheavals… [Yet] it is also true that the most horrible of all new forms of government, whose elements and historical origins I set out to analyze, came no less to an end in Russia with the death of Stalin than totalitarianism came to an end in Germany with the death of Hitler.

III

To repeat in the words of the concluding sentence which Arendt added in 1966: When "Stalin… died…, the story this book has to tell, and the events it tries to understand and come to terms with, came to an at least provisional end" (Arendt 1979: XL). That was how Hannah Arendt summed up the definite limits, within which she wished her concept of total rule to be understood as applicable.

Had a majority of the discipline's scholars adopted her unequivocal stance on the limited duration of total rule – as, for instance, British historian Ian Kershaw did, who identified "sufficient points of contrast" between Stalin's rule and the post-Stalinist Soviet system (Kershaw 1994: 31) –, **a more realistic assessment of the Soviet regime's stability might have ensued which, in its turn, might have left the discipline better prepared for the collapse of the Warsaw Pact states.** In any case, political science would have been spared the larger part of protracted, often long-winded, debates.

Instead, not just Carl Joachim Friedrich stuck to the opinion – at the price of watering down his own defining criteria – that the East European political systems' "totalitarian character" remained untouched by possible "ups and downs" in the actual extent of repression. In 1969, reversing every earlier argument, Friedrich alleged that Stalin's and Hitler's regimes were "nowhere near" typical totalitarian dictatorships. On the contrary, they needed to be considered as "extreme aberrations" (Lietzmann 1999: 145/146). Not unlike Friedrich, German historian Karl Dietrich Bracher even in 1987 invoked the "late totalitarianism" of communist systems which, when deciding to "suffocate" opposition, were proceeding in conformity with mere considerations of expediency (Bracher [1987] in: Jesse 1999: 148).

In contrast to Hannah Arendt's – and Franz Leopold Neumann's – approach, "evolved" theories of totalitarianism such as C. J. Friedrich's emphasized the structures of total rule, rather than the sort of destructiveness that did "not stop short of the pillars of the regime themselves", which Stalinism and Nazism shared (Kershaw 1994: 32). For the National Socialist regime, it may be considered established knowledge that it was not characterized by monopolistic organization and firm hierarchical structures – qualities that stood out in Friedrich's model (Friedrich 1957: 19, 57) -, but rather, as Arendt stresses, by the permanent competition and struggle of despotic subsystems, the rivalry of ever proliferating "action centers" aiming to expand their domain of authority (Broszat [10]1983: 358; also Kershaw 1997: 96).

> It may also be regarded as certain that both regimes pursued "ideological long-term goals" which were to be achieved by "uncontrolled police executive action" (Kershaw, ibid.: 33): The ,totalitarian *state*' is in this sense a misnomer. 'Totalitarianism' has historicallymeant... replacement (of the ,state') by the unmediated subjugation to arbitrary police executive power, justified by recourse to the ideological aims of the Leader.

Ideology and terror, in Hannah Arendt's words. In the Soviet case, documents which have become available since the partial opening of archives, continue to demonstrate die psychological and physical ravages which Arendt attempted to capture – the "traumatic atmosphere of Stalinist terror" ensuing from the "claim to absolute control" (Müller 1991: 10, 15). As will be recalled, the concentration camps, instruments of that terror, were characterised by Arendt as "laboratories" – laboratories in the service of the "experiment" to "make men superfluous", to demonstrate that every human being "can always be replaced" (Arendt 1979: 437/438, 444, 457). Decades-long research into camp conditions under Nazi rule has not arrived at any different result: Treatment by the SS was guided by the principle to degrade the inmates "to the travesty of subhumanity", to demonstrate their utter "worthlessness" in the process of "short-term exploitation" (Pingel 1978: 134, 165).

Yet, as Ian Kershaw has once again pointed out, any concept of totalitarianism – including Hannah Arendt's – is of only limited explanatory value in the comparative analysis of Stalinist and National Socialist rule. Kershaw justifies his reservations against the approach mainly – but not exclusively – by stressing two shortcomings.

On the one hand, the approach does not capture the "large degree of at least partial consensus" which the Nazi regime enjoyed "until deep into the war". And because Nazi terror "was directed at the weaker, discriminated sections of society", it was fatally capable, at least until the unleashing of the war, to even "assist the consensus in building upon existing prejudice". Stalinist terror, in contrast, was directly targeted at "large sections of the population" considered as "real or, increasingly, potential... enemies" either of the collectivisation and industrialisation programs, or of Stalinist despotism (Kershaw, ibid.: 35/36).

On the other hand, Hitler's person and the *Führer* myth constructed around him functioned as Nazism's "unifier", "activator", und "ideological linchpin", making Hitler "irreplaceable" in the context of Nazism's charismatically based authority (Kershaw, ibid.: 37; Kershaw 1997: 101; cf. already Broszat 1970: 402). Stalin rather arose as the "product" of a system of rule which – albeit in different forms – had existed before his rise to power and would live on after his death (Kershaw 1994: 37).

Many elements of Arendt's concept could not be discussed here, not even touched upon, including those which further research has not confirmed. That applies in particular to her hypothesis of the "breakdown of class society" in the crucible of hyperinflation and the Great Depression. Out of that breakdown, those "masses" – according to Arendt – are supposed to have emerged in Germany which then spawned the totalitarian movement (with regard to Russia, compare Benhabib's terse objections against Arendt: Benhabib 2006: 119). However, the Nazi Party's early members and voters must be analysed in terms of specific class affiliations. The party did not grow into a mass movement in an "atomized" society (Hagtvet 1980: 66 ss.). Rather, the Nazis knew how to appeal to the voters emotionally and, by concentrating their attack on the *political* system, to prevent any programmatical debate about diverging *economic and social* interests. Nazism's social pathology hammered home the message that societal conflicts would be transcended "by establishing an enforced racial community" (Winkler 1972: 178/179) of the German "master race [*Herrenrasse*] that, in its own right, takes possession of its part of the globe [*sich ihren Teil an der Welt selbst nimmt*]", as the Pan-German League had asserted as early as 1890.[1] The extent to which the ideological "uprising of 1914", the subsequent "peculiarly German experience of the battle front", finally an aggressive insistence on the illusions destroyed by Germany's defeat had further prepared the terrain for eventual

---

1   The Pan-German proclamation's ("Germany Awaken!") translation in Wertheimer 1924: 31/32 is unreliable, the rendering in Chickering 1984: 43/44 is fragmentary. However, Chickering concludes that "the availability even before the [Great] War of a national symbolism with these aggressive connotations certainly eased the transition to National Socialism after the War" (Chickering 1984: 304).

success of that pathology cannot be discussed here. Distinctive national developments such as these, however, do seem to provide an argument against the analytical usefulness of an approach in terms of totalitarianism – even of the variety which Arendt developed.

A few final sentences regarding the immediate sources which influenced Arendt when she wrote the *Origins* may be appropriate here. I am again referring to the reports on the "dragged-out process of dying" in the camps (Arendt 1979: 446 n. 139) published by Kogon, Rousset, and Zajdlerova. As mentioned before, these were the works of survivors which, in 1946/47, caused Arendt to change the conception of her study quite drastically.

Even a cursory glance will suffice to observe that Arendt's notion of the " "radical evil" perpetrated by total rule, "beyond the pale even of solidarity in human sinfulness" (Arendt 1979: 459) – that this idea derives from the Preface by Eugen Kogon to the original edition of the *SS-Staat*.[2] Kogon's views had been strongly shaped by Catholic doctrine. "Evil", he wrote (Kogon 1946: VI/VII),

> may take forms that one hesitates at putting them down ... I have myself observed, or heard described, scenes which I would prefer to forget not because of their cruelty, but because of the manifest dreadfulness of the evil which they disclosed.

Kogon also emphasized the concentration camps' increasing importance as "SS experimentation fields" for whipping guard units into "experts of brutality devoid of human feeling" by arousing "every instinct of hate, power, and oppression" (Kogon 1946: 5, 6). This emphasis may have inspired Arendt's characterization of the camps as "laboratories" for experimenting in "the realm where 'everything is possible'" (Arendt 1979: 440). Additional consultation of the works by Rousset and Zajdlerova should, in the future, permit us to determine more precisely the extent to which their harrowing memories may have imprinted themselves on Hannah Arendt's concept of total domination. Such consultation should also caution us against applying the concept too easily to political constellations which, to whatever extent we may detest them from the viewpoint of pluralist democracy, do not fit the strict criteria employed by Arendt.

---

2   An abridged translation of the book, titled *The Theory and Practices of Hell*, was published by Farrar, Strauss & Co. in 1950. If Kogon's Preface was omitted, the „Publishers' Introduction to the American Edition" still used parts of his text. The passages translated here from the original were, however, not included.

References

Arendt, Hannah (1979): *The Origins of Totalitarianism*, New York: Harcourt Brace Jovanovich.

Benhabib, Seyla (2006): *Hannah Arendt. Die melancholische Denkerin der Moderne,* Frankfurt: Suhrkamp (2nd enlarged ed.)

Bracher, Karl Dietrich (1987): „Das 20. Jahrhundert als Zeitalter der ideologischen Auseinandersetzungen zwischen demokratischen und totalitären Systemen", in: Eckhard Jesse (ed.): *Totalitarismus im 20. Jahrhundert*, Bonn ²1999, 137-151

Broszat, Martin (1970): „Soziale Motivation und Führerbindung des Nationalsozialismus", *Vierteljahrshefte für Zeitgeschichte* 18, 391-409

Broszat, Martin (¹⁰1983): *Der Staat Hitlers*, München: dtv

Chickering, Roger (1984): *We Men Who Feel Most German. A Cultural Study of the Pan-German League*, Boston: George Allen & Unwin

Friedrich, Carl Joachim (1957): *Totalitäre Diktatur*, Stuttgart: Kohlhammer

Hagtvet, Bernd (1980): "The Theory of Mass Society and the Collapse of the Weimar Republic", in: Stein Larsen et al. (eds.): *Who Were the Fascists?*, Bergen/Oslo: Universitets-forlaget, 66-117

"Inventories of Grief", *Review of Politics* 10 (1948), 136-139

Jänicke, Martin (1971*): Totalitäre Herrschaft. Anatomie eines politischen Begriffs.* Berlin: Duncker & Humblot

Kershaw, Ian (1994): "Totalitarianism Revisted: Nazism and Stalinism in Comparative Perspective", *Tel Aviver Jahrbuch für deutsche Geschichte*, Vol. XXIII, 23-40

Kershaw, Ian (1997): "Working towards the Führer': Reflections on the Nature of the Hitler Dictatorship", in: Ian Kershaw/Moshe Lewin (eds.): *Stalinism and Nazism. Dictatorships in Comparison*, Cambridge/New York: Cambridge University Press, 88-106

Kogon, Eugen (1946): *Der SS-Staat. Das System der deutschen Konzentrationslager*, München: Karl Alber

Lietzmann, Hans J. (1999): *Politikwissenschaft im „Zeitalter der Diktaturen". Die Entwicklung der Totalitarismustheorie Carl Joachim Friedrichs*, Opladen: Leske + Budrich

Lowi, Theodore J. (1967): "The Public Philosophy: Interest-Group Liberalism", *American Political Science Review*, Vol. LXI, 5-24

Ludz, Ursula (2003): „Hannah Arendt und ihr Totalitarismusbuch", in: Antonia Grunenberg (ed.): *Totalitäre Herrschaft und republikanische Demokratie*, Frankfurt a. M.: Peter Lang, 81-92

Müller, Reinhard (1991): „Einführung", in: ders. (ed.): *Die Säuberung. Moskau 1936: Stenogramm einer geschlossenen Parteiversammlung*, Reinbek: Rowohlt, 7-41

Neumann, Franz L. (³1966; ¹1944): *Behemoth. The Structure and Practice of National Socialism*, New York: Harper & Row.

Pingel, Falk (1978): *Häftlinge unter SS-Herrschaft*, Hamburg: Hoffmann & Campe

Schäfer, Gert (1969): „Demokratie und Totalitarismus", in: Gisela Kress/Dieter Senghaas (ed.): *Politikwissenschaft. Eine Einführung in ihre Probleme*, Frankfurt: EVA, 105-154

40

Schäfer, Gert (1993): *Macht und öffentliche Freiheit. Studien zu Hannah Arendt*, Frankfurt: Materialis

Schäfer, Gert (2000): „Denkweg zwischen Tradition und Neubeginn – Hannah Arendt", in: Michael Buckmiller/Dietrich Heimann/Joachim Perels (ed.): *Judentum und politische Existenz. Siebzehn Porträts*, Hannover: Offizin, 385-416

Schmalz-Bruns, Rainer (1995): „Totalitarismustheorie – eine vergessene oder verlassene Stufe der Re flexion", in: Gerhard Lehmbruch (ed.): *Einigung und Zerfall. Deutschland und Europa nach dem Ende des Ost-West-Konflikts.* Opladen: Leske + Budrich, 127-138

Tsao, Roy T. (2003): „The Three Phases of Arendt's Theory of Totalitarianism", in: Antonia Grunenberg (ed.): *Totalitäre Herrschaft und republikanische Demokratie*, Frankfurt a. M.: Peter Lang, 57-79

Wertheimer, Mildred S. (1924): *The Pan-German League 1890-1914*, New York: Columbia University Press

Young-Bruehl, Elisabeth (2002): *Hannah Arendt. For Love of the World*, New Haven/London: Yale University Press

Persisting inequalities of socio-economic and ethno-cultural influence and con-trol – equivalent to so many embedded participatory barriers – have been result-ing in unequal chances for the organized representation of interests and, conse-quently, in limits to more robust redistributive and regulatory public policies. Those limits and those inequalities will, it is safe to note, remain among the ma-jor issues bedeviling 21ˢᵗ-century democracy. And yet, as Robert A. Dahl wrote in concluding his 1989 magnum opus Democracy and its Critics: "The vision of people governing themselves as political equals, and possessing the resources and institutions necessary to do so, will I believe remain a compelling – if always demanding – guide in the search for a society in which people may ... jointly seek the best possible life." To continue exploring the details and problems of that vi-sion is the compelling – normative no less than analytical – task which Robert Dahl has left to our discipline.

Prospects of Pluralist Democracy in an Age of Economic Globalization and World-Wide Migration: A Tribute to Robert A. Dahl

I

Robert A. Dahl died in February, 2014, at the advanced age of 98. He worked for Franklin Delano Roosevelt's New Deal administration during the 1930s, fought in Europe as an infantryman during World War II, finally taught forty years at Yale University. From the mid-1970s, he started raising the norma-tive question how one might proceed "to achieve the best potentialities of pluralist democracy" (Dahl 1982: 170). Subsequently, he would become ever more critical of political inequality and institutional rigidities. Later, Dahl explained his earlier commitment to the ongoing political system by referring to his experience during the Roosevelt period, when labor and agriculture had been recognized as political players alongside business: "The New Deal was not a remote historical episode. It provided grounds for thinking that reform periods would again occur with some frequency" (Dahl/Lindblom 1976: XXX). The pluralism which he expounded during the rest of his career aimed at a more participatory democracy and an employee-controlled economy (see, particularly, Dahl 1989).

Dahl never ceased to emphasize that unequal *social* resources – such as income, education and status – will unavoidably translate into unequal *politi-cal* resources with regard to political activity and control over political agen-da-setting. The lesson which Robert Dahl left us is that reducing disparities in political resources is of prime importance if we wish to ensure the accessibility, the accountability, and – in the final instance – the legitimacy of supposedly 'representative' government. It seems apt that political science should take up Dahl's foremost topic, inquiring how pluralist democracy might be affected by the sweeping changes which, in recent years, have been working on nation-states everywhere.[12]

II

Both in Europe and North America, societies are being transformed from *inside* and *outside,* first by growing economic-financial globalization and permeation, secondly by regional and global migratory movements, which have resulted in increasing ethno-cultural pluralization and diversification. The sovereign power of legislatures is thus being undermined on two fronts.

Compliance with the demands of international investors and with foreign competitive pressures has radically eaten into the use of monetary and fiscal tools by parliaments and governments to regulate national economies. Governmental and market players alike have rivaled each other with neo-liberal recipes for organizing a "slimmed down" state along the lines of private industry, bent on cutting regulation and expenditure, opting for the privatization of public services. The "reform" label has been put to service as a façade for such programs. At the same time, ongoing fiscal and economic globalization definitely did not happen without political intervention. Quite the contrary, it has precisely been pro-market state intervention which has been on the increase (Cerny 1999: 19/20). The mere threat by large transnational corporations of moving capital or economic enterprise of a country has gained so

---

1   See also David Mayhew in a 1997 interview, quoted by Merelman 2003: 85: "Pluralism [was] a New Dealish philosophy".

2   This lecture was given at the University of Zagreb's Political Science Faculty after termination of a conference ("Conceptual Contestation and Political Change") in honor of another distinguished colleague, Ivan Prpic, who, sadly, had also quite recently passed away. I had been privileged to contribute to the conference, talking on Hannah Arendt's concept of total rule (see previous chapter), and I should like to mention here one primary reason for my enduring gratitude to Ivan Prpic: In 1992, he decided to include a translation of my book *Pluralism between Liberalism and Socialism* in the collection *Biblioteka politička misao,* of which he was principal editor (*Pluralizam između liberalizma i socijalizma,* Zagreb: Informator 1991, translated by Mirjana Kasapović). In a new preface written specifically for the occasion, I expressed my hope at the time that the work might contribute by some small part to a spirit of tolerance for different, even controversial positions in the states of former Yugoslavia. However, the capacity for tolerance soon proved exhausted. The tragedies that ensued from there continue to be remembered and presumably to affect the lives of not a few among those surviving today. For that reason, too, it also seems a fitting choice again to reflect on pluralism.

much in credibility that, to prove "competitiveness", welfare states have been "traded down to minimal safety nets" (Hirst 2004: 155). Cutting public outlays reduces resources available for allocation by representatives to constituents, weakening state legitimacy and citizen loyalty to the democratic process (Putzel 2005: 12; Hirst: ibid.).

Due to a largely parallel process of prolonged migratory movements, patterns of societal cleavages and linkages have been changing, with emerging ethnocultural cleavages more often than not exacerbated by – again – economic inequalities. The fragmentation of special interests is being furthered, adherence to traditional institutional loyalties put in jeopardy. Arthur Schlesinger, for one, more than two decades ago sceptically wrote about the "disuniting" of society and polity in the United States by a fundamentalization of group values (Schlesinger 1992). When additional ethnic, religious, and cultural groups are demanding self-determination, self-determination for the polity as a whole may be reduced.

How, then, to accept economic globalization and migration without sacrificing electoral re-sponsiveness and governmental accountability? How to prevent the same issues – grossly unequal distribution of political resources, skewed power structures, structurally embedded participatory barriers – from resurfacing in different contexts?[3] What democratic arrangements are both required and feasible for meeting internal and external challenges, working in the direction of a 'common' (group-related, national, *and* global) good?

A brief retrospect over time may help to further clarify some of the problems which I will be addressing.

When Alexis de Tocqueville visited the pre-Civil War United States more than 150 years ago, he observed an abundance of voluntary associations, governed, as he wrote at the time, by their members' "reason and free will". The French visitor to America, however, also foresaw the decisive contribution of the emerging "large manufacturing establishments" to a new "inequality of conditions" (Tocqueville 1959: 160/161). Increasingly, the joint-stock company came to replace the privately owned and managed firm; increasingly, small enterprises evolved into giant corporations. The extemporaneous assemblies witnessed by Tocqueville were changing, too, developing into large-scale blue collar, white collar and other professional organizations. Governmental interventionism in the economy resulted in ever more formidable administrative bureaucracies: If trade unions and labor parties were pushing governments to assume an active role in stabilizing the economy to prevent cyclical mass unemployment and misery, large corporations in their struggle for security also became interested in governmental regulation. The result was political capitalism, as implemented between the wars and increasingly after World War II (Kolko 1963: 287).

---

3   In Western Europe, the French banlieus, at present, offer a particularly instructive example.

Business, labor and farmer associations developed into unequal partners bargaining for legislative and administrative intervention. Inequality increased further as business organisation continued to evolve: To evade high wages, taxes and restrictive monetary policies, nationally based large enterprises spread their subsidiaries over the world, penetrating other economies and changing into multinational corporations. Four decades before the term "globalisation" gained currency, it was predicted in the early 1970s that the multinational enterprise, without being bound by "any notions of constituency, responsiveness and accountability", would reshape world-wide values and behavior patterns, including prevailing perceptions about the "forms and content" of politics (Osterberg/Ajami 1971).

Empirical research on political involvement has demonstrated widespread individual apathy and alienation existing alongside the institutionalized activities of business corporations and other large associations. We are obviously living in an era characterized by notable discontinuities between the ideal of pluralist democracy and actually prevailing conditions. It is precisely this state of affairs which British political scientist Colin Crouch has labelled "post-democracy" (Crouch 2004: 19 ss.), defining "the major imbalance… between the role of corporate interests and those of virtually all other groups" as "the fundamental cause of democratic decline in contemporary politics" (ibid.: 104). Constrained by such a policy environment, social plurality is translating into political pluralism to a diminishing extent.

Having emphasized these predicaments, we have still not arrived at the end of knotty political problems and thorny issues. Learning "to live with the public expression and institutionalization of ethnocultural diversity" may justly be considered, as Canadian political philosopher Will Kymlicka and Eastern European expert Magda Opalski have jointly noted, a further key precondition for any "stable and just democracy" (Kymlicka/Opalski 2001: 1). Both made their observation after the civil wars in the Balkan countries had shocked the world with the atrocities of "ethnic cleansing". Taking into account the warning provided by that experience – how to promote the further ethnocultural "pluralization" of already existing societal pluralities without inviting the fundamentalization of group values?

To accommodate enduring ethnocultural differences, a politics of recognition and inclusion is required which must attempt to steer a delicate course between cultural fragmenti-zation and forcible assimilation. Any such politics unavoidably implies limiting the political power of ethnocultural *majorities*. Just as minorities have been doing, however, these majorities may (re)discover ethnicity as a source of belonging, of identity, of ostensible "certainty in an uncertain world" Durando 1993: 26) – particularly when bedeviled by economic anxieties and ideological disorientation.

Clearly, new inequalities and conflicts are interacting with old inequalities and conflicts. The relationship between societal plurality and political pluralism "becomes more and more complex and problematic", as plurality is augmented, while pluralism is potentially undermined. On the one hand, the transformation of plurality into pluralist practices requires supportive structural, institutional, even mental factors. On the other hand, that process will always face contestation by embedded inequalities, clashing norms, new claimants (Cerny 2006: 88, 91, 110).

III

"Pluralist democracy" is a term at once positive (descriptive) and normative (prescriptive). Descriptively, it refers to the existence of a plurality of interests and corresponding groups which, as latent centers of power, may (and are permitted to) organize into associations. Normatively, the notion endorses the transformation of this diversity into public policies shaping society by a process of conflict, negotiation and compromise, on condition that individual rights are respected and constitutional rules of the game apply.

After World War II, pluralist democracy was supposed to exist in Western-type capitalist countries, particularly in the United States as it had emerged from the New Deal reforms. Even so, American pluralists, particularly Robert Dahl and Charles Lindblom, conceded that capitalist democracies offered "unusual opportunities" for "pyramiding" resources such as income, education and status into structures of political influence and political power (Dahl/Lindblom 1953: 315, 329; Dahl 1963: 227).

Looking for ways "to achieve the best potentialities of pluralist democracy" (Dahl 1982: 170), Dahl and Lindblom singled out the large business corporation as the major target for structural, participatory reforms. "Nothing", they argued, "could be less appropriate than to consider the giant firm a *private* enterprise" – because whether you look at sales, at assets, at the number of employees, or at the impact of corporate pricing, investment, or financing policies, business corporations have developed into *social and public* institutions (Dahl/Lindblom 1976: XXVIII/XXIX; Dahl 1970: 119/120). They have, in fact, acquired political dimensions. Suggesting that the executives of large corporations are subject neither to effective internal control by stockholders, nor to adequate external control by governments and markets, Dahl went on to propose a determined effort at further democratization – the "enfranchisement" of blue- and white-collar employees, realizing economic democracy. *If you buy government bonds, you do not control government policy – so why should investors be entitled to govern the firms in which they invest?* Control should, therefore, be transferred to those who would be able to effectively exercise it – to the employees (Dahl 1982: 199, 204; Dahl 1989: 327 ss., 331/332).

Such spill-over of democratic norms from polity onto economy would, of course, be diametrically opposed to present neo-liberal ideas about reorganizing the state as a quasi-enterprise association. The adjective "political" would henceforth relate to any form of group decision-making. Such pluralistic democratization would be intended to reduce disparities in control over political resources, to secure the more equitable representation of social interests by broad political participation and, in the last instance, to make democratic governments more responsive and more accountable to their voters.

The recent, barely overcome financial and economic crisis not only demonstrates the need for a return to more robust regulatory policies. To secure citizens' loyalty to the democratic process and their political commitment, a determined effort at economic democratization should be put high on the agenda of our thinking about democracy.

IV

When the term "cultural pluralism" was first introduced by Horace Kallen in 1924, immigrant subcultures were flourishing in the eastern United States, after nearly 15 million immigrants – mostly from Southern and Eastern Europe – had been admitted to the United States between 1900 and 1920 (see Menand 2001: 381). Arguing against assimilationist pressure and "melting pot" conformity, Kallen offered his vision of a "commonwealth of different cultures" (Kallen 1924: 11, 116). Convinced that society's creativity would benefit from different ethnocultural strains, he proposed granting equal treatment to every such tradition. Affirmative action procedures (which means favoring members of a disadvantaged group in selection processes for education and employment positions), introduction of official multilingualism, a composition of political bodies reflecting the existence of various ethnic groups may work to reinforce cultural pluralism.

Conversely, public policies may remain neutral toward ethnocultural differences. Within such a framework, discrimination on ethnic grounds is legally prohibited; benefits are provided according to *individual* eligibility. The unit of attribution for equity considerations is always and irrevocably the individual.

During the 1980s and 90s, and into the 21st century, most of the debate has been centering on these policy alternatives (see Bellamy/Hollis 1999). So far, the discussion has achieved nothing which even remotely resembles conceptual clarity. The extent of differential treatment to be accorded to ethnic groups in order to protect and develop their special cultural characteristics is and remains controversial. This includes the extent of self-determination and of participation in the larger society as corporate bodies with political status and rights. Should liberal principles and procedures, developed as a guard against the power of majorities over minorities, be reinterpreted in favor of ethnocultural groups, or is there insufficient reason to modify the liberal emphasis on *individual* rights (Kukathas 1997: 230)? Obviously, groups as well as states may violate individual human rights. Would not any determined movement in the direction of group rights prevent individuals from "opting out" of their group by adopting ideas and practices running counter to their own ethnocultural heritage?

Should not, for these reasons, compromises rather than clear-cut solutions be sought? Countries such as India, post-apartheid South Africa, Canada, Belgium or Switzerland offer a wide array of varying, more or less successful models. Available options (which, of course, may overlap) include legal protection and public funding for the expression of cultural pecularities; federalism as a form of self-government; finally the more complex arrangements of consociationalism, meaning group-based political representation.

It is this latter regime of consociational governance which has been attracting increasing attention (see Kymlicka 1995: chs. 2, 7). Put in optimistic terms, group-based representation may result in the ability of "the state to offer an emotional identity counterbalancing the emotional loyalties to ethnic and religious communities, thereby preventing the fragmentation of society into narrow, selfish communalism" (Modood 1999: 88). Would a high degree of group-based political representation indeed meet expectations of contributing to a more – not less – vibrant democracy?

Consociationalism includes the following basic elements (see Lijphart 1977: 25): Considerable autonomy for each involved group in the management of its internal affairs; application of a proportional standard in political representation, in civil service appointments, and in the allocation of financial resources; right of mutual veto in governmental decision-making; finally and decisively, joint government by an either official or unofficial grand coalition of group leaders.

A case study of consociational democracy in the Netherlands during the 1950s and 1960s has spelled out a number of significant negative consequences (see Lijphart 1968: 111, 129, 131) – elite predominance, the arcane character of negotiations, a large measure of political immobilism. Such immobilism may "entrench an unjust *status quo*" (Lijphart 1977: 51), leading to morally reprehensible deadlocks. At an even more basic level, group autonomy (as I already indicated earlier) may involve internal restrictions on the rights of individual members "to dissent from traditional practices" (Kymlicka 1995: 154), thus running counter to liberal-democratic conceptions of minority rights.

There exists no general answer to the question how far the serious disadvantages of consociationalism may be offset, except in the case of severely divisional cleavages, which could lead to either dictatorship or civil war. In any case, growing ethnocultural demands in ever more countries suggest that the load on democratic political systems to accommodate the diversity of minority groups will be increasing.

V

Any democracy will continue to require, first and foremost, "resourceful" individuals – by which are meant, quite literally, individuals committed to *pluralist* orientations *and* with increasing, rather than decreasing, access to political resources. In the last instance, the uncertain future of pluralist democracy will be determined by a political culture which puts a premium on the educated citizen, prepared *and* able (resources!) to involve him- or herself.

To the extent that societal (definitely including ethnocultural) and political groupings maintain democratic practices internally, they significantly contribute to such a political culture through the transfer of norms and values. To the extent, on the other hand, that both groups with democratic practices and involved individuals should be found increasingly few and far between, solutions for the persistent problem what it might mean to live democratically will become anything but easier.

Last but far from least, a political science is needed which, by a determined effort, redresses its present "neglect of the citizen" attested by 2009 Economics Nobel Laureate Elinor Ostrom (see Toonen 2010: 197).[4] By being critical of power structures skewed in favor of either politically and economically privileged minorities, or of ethnically privileged majorities, political science should help prepare citizens for civic involvement. Pursuing research and teaching in a humanist spirit, it should emphasize broad societal participation in the shaping of public policies.[5]

Adressing relevant issues requires the *re-emergence of normative notions* as an indispensable part of the discipline, though definitely not at the cost of empirical rigor in researching constraints and perspectives. Put in a nutshell: Political science should again develop visions about how a "good society" might be designed – and how it might be politically brought even remotely closer to being attained. Such a discipline might then work as a science of democracy – as Robert Dahl intended it should do.

---

4 Ostrom tragically died of cancer in 2012, before she could address – as had been planned – the XXII IPSA World Congress of Political Science in Madrid. .

5 See also this author's article: „How Political Science Might Regain Relevance and Obtain an Audience: A Manifesto for the 21st Century", *European Political Science* 10 (2011), 220-225, reprinted in: Rainer Eisfeld: *Radical Approaches to Political Science. Roads Less Traveled*, Leverkusen/Toronto 2012, 13-19.

References

Bellamy, Richard/Hollis, Martin (eds., 1999): *Pluralism and Liberal Neutrality*, London/Portland

Bellamy, Richard/Hollis, Martin (1999): "Consensus, Neutrality and Compromise" in: Bellamy/Hollis, op. cit., 54-78

Cerny, Philip G. (1999): "Globalization and the Erosion of Democracy", *European Journal of Political Research*, 36, 1-26

Cerny, Philip G. (2006): "Plurality, Pluralism and Power: Elements of Pluralisrt Analysis in an Age of Globalization", in: Rainer Eisfeld (ed.): *Pluralism: Developments in the Theory and Practice of Democracy*, Leverkusen/Farmington Hills, 81-110

Crouch, Colin (2004): *Post-Democracy*, Cambridge

Dahl, Robert A. (1963): *Who Governs?*, New Haven/London

Dahl, Robert A. (1970): *After the Revolution? Authority in a Good Society*, New Haven

Dahl, Robert A. (1982): *Dilemmas of Pluralist Democracy*, New Haven

Dahl, Robert A. (1989): *Democracy and its Critics*, New Haven

Dahl, Robert A./Lindblom, Charles E. (1953): *Politics, Economics and Welfare*, Chicago

Dahl, Robert A./Lindblom, Charles E. (1976): "Preface" to Re-Issue of Dahl/Lindblom, op. cit., XXI-XLIV

Durando, Dario (1993): "The Rediscovery of Identity", *Telos*, No. 97, 117-144

Hirst, Paul (2004): "What is Globalization?", in: Engelstad, Fredrik/Østerud, Øyvind (eds.): *Power and Democracy*, Aldershot, 151-168

Kallen, Horace M. (1924): *Culture and Democracy in the United States*, New York

Kolko, Gabriel (1963): *The Triumph of Conservatism*, Glencoe

Kukathas, Chandran (1997): "Are There Any Cultural Rights", in: Kymlicka (ed.), op. cit., 228-256

Kymlicka, Will (1995): *Multicultural Citizenship*, Oxford/New York

Kymlicka, Will/Opalski, Magda (eds.) (2001): *Can Liberal Pluralism be Exported?*, Oxford/New York

Lijphart, Arend (1968): *The Politics of Accommodation*, Berkeley/Los Angeles

Lijphart, Arend (1977): *Democracy in Plural Societies*, New Haven/London

Merelman, Richard M. (2003): *Pluralism at Yale*, Madison/London: University of Wisconsin Press

Modood, Tariq (1999): "Multiculturalism, Secularism and the State", in: Bellamy/Hollis (eds.), op. cit., 79-97

Osterberg, David/Ajami, Fouad (1971): "The Multinational Corporation: Expanding the Frontiers of World Politics", *Journal of Conflict Resolution* 15, 457-470

Putzel, James (2005): "Globalization, Liberalization, and Prospects for the State", *International Political Science Review* 26, 5-16

Schlesinger, Arthur M. (1992): The Disuniting of America, New York/London

Tocqueville, Alexis de (1959): *Democracy in America*, New York

Toonen, Theo (2010): "Resilience in Public Administration: The Work of Elinor and Vincent Ostrom from a Public Administration Perspective", *Public Administration Review* 70, 193-202

Nominated by the German Political Science Association, Klaus von Beyme received the Mattei Dogan High Achievement Award at the 2012 World Congress of Political Science, held by IPSA in Madrid. The nomination was supported by ten other national associations across Europe – quite literally, from the Balkans to the Baltic, and from Spain to Russia –, attesting to the high esteem in which Beyme is held. To quote a single sentence from the Hungarian Political Science Federation's support letter, signed by its president Zsolt Enyedi: "Beyme's works have socialized generations of scholars into political science." A life-time achievement could hardly be characterized in more appropriate terms. It was my pleasure and privilege to deliver the address paying tribute to Beyme, whom I have known as a scholar for over 30 years, and whom I have never ceased to like personally and to respect professionally.

Klaus von Beyme: The Political Scientist as Global Scholar and Public Intellectual

I

In analysing politics from Madrid to Moscow, Klaus von Beyme once wrote that he had let himself be guided by the principle to treat each country with as much empathy as his own. No wonder: Beyme is fluent in seven, and his works have been translated into ten languages, including Chinese, Korean, Polish, Croatian, Slovenian, Italian, Greek, and Spanish – English as a matter of course. He has written on political theories and political systems (those of the United States, Soviet Russia, Spain, Italy, and Germany – the latter work, several times updated, has meanwhile seen 10 printings), on Central-East Europe's transition from Communism, on interest groups, political parties and comparative politics, on policy fields such as health, traffic and residential construction. And he has devoted an increasing amount of sophisticated thinking to ways in which political science relates to the social and cultural world around it, with a focus on architecture and on art. Anyone intent on broadening their field of inquiry beyond the discipline's traditional limits, may draw encouragement from him.

Beyme was the first West German exchange student to be enrolled in Moscow during the late 1950s, and he went on to distinguish himself as a Research Fellow at Harvard University's Russian Research Center. Just two years ago, Lomonosov University made him Honorary Professor for his significant contributions both to the development of political science and to relations between the Moscow-based university and its German counterparts. For seven years, Beyme served on the Research Council of the European University Institute in Florence. He was a Fellow both at the Wissenschaftskolleg Berlin and at the Maison des Sciences de l'Homme in Paris. Holder of an honorary doctorate from Berne University in Switzerland, a former president of the German Political Science Association in the 1970s and of IPSA in the early 1980s, Beyme is a rare example of the political scientist as global scholar and public intellectual.

A public intellectual has been defined as one who seeks to advance both knowledge and human freedom. Beyme has always been extremely reticent to publicly acknowledge his fundamentally humanist orientation. But he did, on occasion, refer to the impressions deeply imprinted on his memory of fleeing, as a 10-year old boy, from the burning city of Breslau, only to find the city of Halberstadt, upon his arrival, also in flames. Small wonder that he concluded a 1987 work on post-World War II architecture and urban development policies in the two German states with a remarkably unequivocal sentence: "The surviving Germans' sense of having escaped, in the Second World War, by the skin of their teeth needs to be transformed into the awareness that, in a Third World War, peoples would lose more than their cities' visual identity."

Even before he became IPSA President, Beyme supported the idea of bringing the German Democratic Republic into the IPSA fold. At the time, the East German delegates were still performing minor miracles when traveling to IPSA conferences: They boarded their plane as jurists, economists or philosophers, exiting it as political scientists. "Change through closer ties" was Beyme's often affirmed policy. He and Secretary General John Trent even found a face-saving formula that allowed the Republic of China – at least for half a decade – to join IPSA without alienating Taiwan.

II

His colleague Wolfgang Merkel once remarked about Beyme that "his theoretical creativity has always been constrained by the scruples of his enormous historical and empirical knowledge". Beyme's 1994 work on *System Transformation in Eastern Europe*, translated into English and Korean – another divided nation –, stands as a perfect example of a work saturated with conceptional and historical insight and sophisticated observation. Every such study would have looked at institution-building, dealt with social and ethnic cleavages and their effects on the establishment of political parties, focused on the daunting problem of synchronizing political and economic transformation. Beyme went beyond.

He provided an incisive analysis of "transformation without elite exchange" in the areas of administration, the economy, academe (excepting the former GDR), but also in politics, particularly in Albania, Bulgaria, Romania, Serbia, and Russia. He argued that the concept of civil society, developed as a counter-ideology to actually existing socialism, reflected not a few intellectuals' anti-political stance and their lack of familiarity with economic matters. In Beyme's opinion, the notion's idealistic features were poorly suited to the often harsh new political and economic realities. He identified nationalism as a much more potent force for providing political legitimation and psychological gratifications under conditions of economic downturn, and he correctly foresaw that it was nationalism which, for a considerable period, would fill the ideological vacuum. Beyme's account of ethnic policies under socialism – "culminating in the right to establish folk dance groups", as he ironically notes –, their mobilising post-1989 consequences, and a few beginnings of new minority policies – that account is among his book's most perceptive chapters.

In another masterful, tightly argued chapter, linking the three dimensions of the political – polity, politics, and policies –, Beyme explored the complex processes which had steadily eroded the legitimacy of the socialist system. As he has also emphasized time and again, however, the discipline had absolutely failed to predict the collapse of existing socialism, and theories of totalitarianism, with their emphasis on terror and coercion, had hindered rather than helped any attempts at assessing future developments. Different paradigms had not prevented their advocates either from making false assumptions. Here Beyme was characteristically candid; he himself had preferred the interest group approach pioneered by Gordon Skilling. Ever the skeptical realist, Beyme maintained then and remains convinced to this day:

Political science cannot predict processes on the macro-level. Neither the student rebellion, nor the oil crisis, nor finally the rise of fundamentalism were forecast by the discipline. "Informed guesswork", according to Beyme, is the best we can expect.

III

Comparative Political Science, his latest book published two years ago, assembles 21 articles and chapters from the past decade in three sections – "Comparing Theories", "Comparing Institutions", "Comparing Policies". These pieces attest to Beyme's undiminished intellectual curiosity and creativity. As an example, a single chapter must suffice here: A tightly structured review of five decades of German health policy, covering the visions and the conundrums, the decisions and the non-decisions, attempts at regulation and the barriers against such efforts, the interplay of historical inheritances, institutional structures and organized interests. These mere ten pages impress the reader as nothing short of brilliant.

Of the volume's chapters, three focus on cultural and art policy. When Klaus von Beyme began writing about culture and politics in 1987, he started out with a book on the part played by architecture and urban planning in the process of rebuilding the two Germanys after 1945 , arguing that "no field of art is as strongly impregnated politically as architecture and urban development". More such works followed: on German cultural policy; on *The Art of Power and the Countervailing Power of Art*; on *Age of Avantgardes: Art and Society, 1905-1955*; finally on *Fascination of the Exotic: Exoticism, Racism and Sexism in Art*.

The Art of Power and the Countervailing Power of Art contained the gist of Beyme's considerations on the relationship between art, polity and politics. I quote:

> Since the Renaissance, politics increased its autonomy by a symbiosis with art, which served the aesthetic legitimation of authority ... In democracies with universal suffrage and parliamentary responsibility of governments, art and power abandoned that temporary symbiosis and began growing apart ... Nowadays, aesthetical orchestration of politics pushes aside art as a technique for legitimating authority ... To the extent that the state promotes art only marginally ..., economics finds its way into art production.

In a chapter on "Architecture in the Service of Awe and Intimidation", Beyme identified early modern monumentalism as an expression of agonistic societal pluralism and subsequent 20th century sites for mass rallies of indoctrinated crowds as a distinguishing feature of totalitarian dictatorships. In another chapter on "The October Revolution's Political Myths in the Arts", he argued that "mythologizing the collective" had been the revolution's most important integrative mechanism, on which Stalin had later been able to build his show trials.

IV

In 2008, Klaus von Beyme received the Schader Foundation Award, one of the most important German awards given to social scientists, for distinguishing himself in the "dialog between the social sciences and practical life". Beyme's work provides an enduring incentive not to settle for political studies in the sense of a reductionist science focused on the "management" of parliamentary and party government. Rather, political scientists should sharpen their minds and open their hearts to addressing those pressing national, regional and global challenges which transcend any self-imposed confines of our discipline. In concluding, I would like to refer to just a single instance indicating issues of the kind which a political science informed by Klaus von Beyme's example might address more widely.

In his treatise on world poverty and human rights, Yale political philosopher Thomas Pogge has argued that Western political and financial institutions are deeply implicated in keeping the corrupt and oppressive rulers of impoverished states in power, due to the interest of affluent democracies in obtaining access to natural resources and in issuing lucrative loans. Pogge's essays contain enough material which the discipline might debate with a view to speaking out in favour of a more just and more equitable organization of political processes and institutions, both nationally and internationally.

I am profoundly convinced that awarding the Mattei Dogan Prize to Klaus von Beyme for his outstanding achievements will provide a powerful boost to the kind of political science which does not shy away from incorporating historical dynamics, societal conflicts, and embedded power relations, and which supports men and women – wherever they may live – in their quest to participate more effectively, more knowledgeably, more freely in today's political decision-making.

Two Profoundly Different Schools of Political Science

Having been forced into exile by the Nazis in 1933, DHfP lecturer Franz Leopold Neumann (later the author of Behemoth) studied at LSE under Harold J. Laski, obtaining a second doctorate. Might one infer that the Berlin Institute and the London School were, to some extent, kindred institutions? Exploring and contrasting their emergence and evolution rather reveals pronounced differences, reflecting political and cultural environments that diverged as widely. After WW II, when the DHfP was re-launched, Germany's defeat had changed the context drastically. Political science was now pursued "from a Weimar perspective" (Klaus Günther), intended to draw lessons from Germany's recent past. At LSE, an "absence" (Dahrendorf) of empirical studies would even longer characterize the discipline. The following lecture was given in Mexico City in 2013 and published in Poland a year later – testimony to a continuing international interest in looking at the pursuit of political science from a comparative perspective.

Political Science in Great Britain and Germany: The Roles of LSE and DHfP

I

The London School of Economics and Political Science (LSE) and the Deutsche Hochschule für Politik (DHfP, German Political Studies Institute) in Berlin both emerged extramurally. LSE was founded in 1895 by Fabian Socialists Sidney and Beatrice Webb. The DHfP was established in 1920 by liberal-national publicists Ernst Jäckh and Theodor Heuss. Superficial resemblances ended there, however: The founders' aims differed markedly; incorporation into London and Berlin universities occurred at different times and in different ways.

The chair of political science set up at LSE in 1914 was held, until 1950, by two reform-minded Fabians, Graham Wallas and Harold Laski. The DHfP, which did not win academic recognition during the 1920s, split into nationalist, "functionalist", and democratic "schools". Against that backdrop, the chapter will discuss Harold Laski's magnum opus (1925) *A Grammar of Politics* as an attempt at offering a vision of the "good society", and Theodor Heuss' 1932 study *Hitler's Course* as an example of the divided Hochschule's inability to provide adequate analytical assessments both of the Nazi movement and of the gradual infringement, by established elites, of the Weimar constitution.

Laski's work and intellectual legacy reinforced the tendency toward a predominance, in British political science, of normative political theory. West

German political science, initially pursued "from a Weimar perspective", was also conceived as a highly normative enterprise emphasizing classical political theory, the institutions and processes of representative government, and the problematic ideological and institutional predispositions peculiar to German political history. Against that background, the chapter will look, one the one hand, at the contribution to "New Left" thinking (1961 ff.) by Ralph Miliband, who studied under Laski and taught at LSE until 1972, and at Paul Hirst's 1990s theory of associative democracy, which builds on Laski's pluralism. On the other hand, the text will consider Karl Dietrich Bracher's seminal work *The Disintegration of the Weimar Republic* (1955) and Ernst Fraenkel's 1964 collection *Germany and the Western Democracies* which originated, respectively, from the (Research) Institute for Political Science, added to Berlin's Free University in 1950, and the DHfP, re-launched in the same year.

In a brief concluding section, the paper will touch on the reception, both in Great Britain and West Germany, of the approaches of "modern" American political science since the mid-1960s.

II

The Fabian Society was set up as an intellectual circle in 1884 by, among others, the two Webbs, George Bernard Shaw and Graham Wallas. Inspiration for its name came from Fabius Maximus Cunctator, the cautious Roman warlord of the Second Punic War. The Fabians' avowed principles were "permeation", "gradualism", and "municipal socialism". Permeation meant the attempt "at incalculat(ing) Socialist thought and Socialist projects into the minds not merely of … political Liberals or Radicals, but also of political conservatives" (Webb 1920: XXVI). Gradualism, which stood for constitutional, "respectable" socialism, was added after the formation of the Labour Party, in which the Society took part. Both principles found expression in a veritable stream of tracts, lectures, commission reports, and proposals for specific legislative or administrative measures, particularly ("bottom-up") on the municipal level. The Fabians influenced the British Labour Party to an extraordinary degree. In 1918, Sidney Webb wrote the party's revised program. After a generation, more than half of the just under 400 Labour MPs elected in 1945 were Fabians (Beveridge 1952: V) – even if it has been cautioned that this "was just one of the things one 'did' as a Labour activist, like being a member of Co-operatives UK" (Grant 2013: Personal Communication).

Founding the London School of Economics and Political science was made possible by windfall money: a 20,000 GBP bonanza ("the equivalent of nearly 1 mio. pounds a hundred years later": Dahrendorf 1995: 3) bequeathed to the Fabian Society in 1894 by a supporter who, despairing of a severe illness, took his life. The Webbs' and others' motives (among them Bertrand Russell) have been summarized by Ralf Dahrendorf, much later the LSE's director, as "the five E's" (Dahrendorf 1995: 29-46): advanced *education* for practical purposes, following the model provided by the Ecole libre des sciences politiques established in Paris two decades earlier; *economics* offering, once again, practical advice for current affairs; *equality* through benevolent social reform and determined collective action; *efficiency* in the application of modern science, aimed at furthering administrative competence and superior expertise; finally, somewhat surprisingly, *empire,* the notion that economic imperialism and social reform might serve as a good combination.

In Germany, an extramural Political Studies Institute, free of the rigid constraints of the country's traditional system of higher education, was twice during the 20th century considered the adequate response to the perceived need of politically educating the German people. In 1920 as in 1949, it would be located in Berlin, and would at the outset resemble an adult education establishment offering evening classes. In 1949, after degeneration into Nazism, it was hoped that political education would "help in providing, with regard to information and comportment, the underpinnings required by a fresh start in democratic politics" (Blanke et al. 1975: 54). Less so in 1920, after Germany had suffered unexpected defeat in World War I. According to Theodor Heuss, first Director of Studies at the DHfP – much later, of course, also the German Federal Republic's first president –, German politics, "forced into a system of humiliations by external force and through its own fault, (knew) but one issue: the struggle for national liberation" (Heuss 1921: 33/34).

Ernst Jäckh, the DHfP's first and only president, did not mince words either when pronouncing himself in favour of an institute that would provide "a focal point around which to crystallize a new Germany and, thereby, a new Europe imbued with a new spirit (albeit not the pointless, brutal 'spirit' of Versailles)" – referring, of course, to the Versailles Peace Treaty and the constraints it imposed on Germany (Jäckh 1921: 31). After 1945, Jäckh would omit the part about "the pointless, brutal 'spirit' of Versailles" from reprints of his earlier speech (Jäckh 1952: 14; id. 1960: 87/88). At the time, however, the revisionist impulse was unmistakable.

The necessary money was initially provided, first and foremost, by the new governments of Germany – usually referred to as the Weimar Republic, named after the city where a constituent assembly had drafted the new constitution – and of the state of Prussia, supplemented by grants from a few liberal industrialists such as Bosch or Siemens. After 1926/27, further financial support came from the Rockefeller Foundation and the Carnegie Endowment for International Peace.

Among the institute's tasks, Jäckh and Heuss included training for the Civil Service and the education of future political "leaders". In addition to the conviction held by large segments of the population and certainly by an overwhelming majority among the Weimar Republic's prominent political and academic players, that the peace treaty concluding World War I had been unjust and needed to be revised, a second theme was running through the Weimar Republic's political debates: that, in a parliamentary democracy, the selection and training of capable political leaders constituted *the* major problem. Such over-emphasis on leadership did not least derive from Germany's authoritarian past. During the 1920s, the leadership ideal came to acquire almost "metaphysical significance" in Germany. Before long, it would be tied to "great-man doctrines", favouring an anti-parliamentary and antidemocratic backlash even among self-styled "republicans by force of reason" (Struve 1973: 9; Döring 1975: 231; Faulenbach 1980: 310).

Thus, in the last instance, differences between the two extramural facilities, LSE and DHfP, could hardly have been more marked. Five years after LSE had been set up, a new constitution gave an economics and political science faculty to the University of London, recognizing LSE as a university school (Dahrendorf 1995: 32, 56/57). The DHfP would have to wait more than half a century for a similar development to occur.

III

No wonder that highly different approaches to political science emerged at LSE and DHfP. A chair of political science was established at the London School in 1914. Until 1950, it was successively held by two reform-minded Fabians, Graham Wallas and Harold Laski, whom informed opinion has included among the half dozen or so "founding fathers" of British political science (Kavanagh 2003: 594).

Wallas viewed the "great society", which had sprung "from steam and electricity", as characterized by impersonal, mechanistic relations (Dewey 1954: 96). Because individuals are affected by "remote, obscure" environments not adequately understood and controlled, they find it difficult to plan their lives. This situation is aggravated by the fact that employment conditions, "often confined to highly repetitive operations", tend to suppress special skills and to narrow perspectives (Heslep 1968: 156). Wallas suggested that employees should work in small groups whose members might interact with each other (ibid.: 157), an idea that has remained essential to concepts of industrial democracy. Schooling should be universal, working hours short, women "enfranchised" politically, socially, economically.

Some of his other reform proposals sounded rather technocratic. Specialized experts should cooperate with legislators, bureaucrats, representatives of the professions and labor unions in "planning" society, including programs for spacious housing, parks and forest areas, even park benches (ibid.: 157/158). Disqualifying such policies as analogous to later fascist "strength through joy" programs would, however, miss the point. Wallas was essentially a moralist, intent on curbing drunkenness, disorderly conduct, violence which resulted from tensions and unhappiness.

When Harold Laski was appointed Wallas' successor in 1926, he was on his way to becoming, during the 1930s, "the most important socialist intellectual in the English-speaking world"; already by 1922, a "utopian character" introduced by H. G. Wells in his novel *Men Line Gods* bore the name Laski (Kramnick/Sheerman 1993: 1/2). He had previously taught at McGill (Montreal) for two, at Harvard for another four years as an instructor and tutor, and had held a lectureship at LSE for six more years. Borrowing the term "pluralistic" from the philosophy of William James, he had, in a 1915 lecture delivered at Columbia University, introduced it into political theory.

The ideas of the Fabian Society had considerably influenced Laski's thinking. So, for a time, had the argument of the guild socialists – "young rebels" in the Fabians' ranks who held that self-government was identical with representation according to the differentiation of functions on every social level, definitely including the factory and the enterprise. Convinced that "no political democracy (could) be real" without being underpinned "by an economic democracy" (Laski 1919: 38), Laski initially envisioned two participatory machineries – a vocational congress of producers and a territorial parliament of consumers – which would exist side by side, posing major practical problems of coordination.

Laski's 1925 magnum opus *A Grammar of Politics* offered both a textbook on political science and a vision of the "good society". From his previous work, he retained two central contentions:

> The structure of social organization involves, not myself and the state, my groups and the state, but all these and their interrelationships... The interest of the community is the total result of the whole pressure of social forces (Laski 1925: 141, 261).

> Exactly as the evolution of political authority has been concerned with the erection of limitations upon the exercise of power, so also with economic authority... In a sense not less urgent than that in which Lincoln used it, no state can survive that is half-bond and half-free. The citizen... must be given the power to share in the making of those decisions which affect him as a producer if he is... to maximize his freedom (ibid.: 112/113).

However, Laski now repudiated the guild socialist project on the grounds that its institutional difficulties would be "insurmountable" (ibid.: 72). Instead, he focused on that distinction which has remained pivotal to conceptions of democratizing society – the separation of property from control (ibid.: 112):

> Just as the holder of government bonds has no control... over government policy, so it is possible to prevent interference with the direction of an industrial enterprise by the loaners thereto of capital... The present system of private property does not in the least involve the present technique of industrial direction.

In his liberal and socialist commitment both to civil liberties and to "the replacement of economic individualism... by an egalitarian society based on cooperation and public service" (Kramnick/Sheerman 1993: 3), Laski's "political pluralism used socialism to shape a new interpretation for liberalism" (Griffith 1933: 78). It required the Great Depression of 1929 and the circumstances of the formation of the British National Government in 1932 for Laski to move more clearly in a Marxian direction without, however, as has been erroneously suggested, "rejecting" pluralism (Deane 1955: 153). Rather, by combining pluralism and Marxism, he proposed in 1937 to transcend the capitalist system, envisaging not violent action but, in a term Laski was to coin during World War II, a "revolution by consent".

Wallas and particularly Laski typified the emerging discipline of political science in Britain which was considered "part of a humane tradition, deeply rooted in the classics", wherein prescriptive political theory "maintained a leading role", and whose teachers, as a rule, "were public intellectuals" not "shy(ing) away from political engagement". Also, LSE and Oxford (Cambridge to a lesser extent) continued to function as inter-war centers for the study of politics (Kelly 2010: VII; Kavanagh 2003: 594, 600, 610; Grant 2010: 12, 14).

The political and social context favored such a rather unbroken development. British political tradition and political institutions went largely unchallenged. The Great Reform of 1832 had established the principle of gradual transition to representative democracy, to which the major political parties had increasingly subscribed. *Against that backdrop,* **projects of further democratization**, *such as those considered by Laski, might reasonably be envisaged.*

In Germany, belated unification had been achieved by Prussian arms under Junker command, rather than by an ascending middle class bent on establishing civil liberty and governmental responsibility. After Imperial Germany's defeat in 1918, not merely detractors of the republic continued to nurse aspirations to recapture the country's pre-war position of power on the continent. In theory as in practice, such revisionism reinforced a functional, instrumentalist approach to both domestic and foreign policy. If democratic government, if the League of Nations proved unable to achieve revision, both might be expendable – which meant that, *in German political science, the* **very principle of democracy was coming under attack.**

At the DHfP, the functional perception of democracy as merely a (more or less adequate) method of government, and of international conciliation as primarily a tool for achieving revision would, during the final stages of the Weimar Republic, provide an opening for the endorsement of authoritarian "solutions" to Germany's political crisis. On top of that, a growing element among the Berlin Institute's faculty – self-styled "conservative revolutionaries", as they referred to themselves – subscribed to a radicalized, nationalist version of revisionism, unwilling, as they proclaimed, "to let the fatherland perish by the hands of inadequate leaders and external enemies" (Spahn 1925 : 3). Increasingly from 1927, the DHfP's positions and publications were opened to those intransigent nationalist enemies of the Weimar Republic, whose approach centered on four basic tenets:

A "homogeneous" nation, rooted in "blood and soil", distinct from "atomistic" and "divisive" modern society; a corporatist, supposedly "organic" state, replacing "mechanistic" Western parliamentarism; a belief in authoritarian political leadership, as opposed to democratic "leveling"; finally, the perspective of renewed German hegemony in central Europe as a "continuing German mission". This approach amounted to politicized, rather than political science. Inevitably, it paved the way for the Nazi doctrine that no science could escape being political science – in the sense that it had to serve purposes laid down by political, i. e. Nazi, authorities.

The institute split along conceptual lines into nationalist, functionalist, and democratic "schools". In contrast to the functionalists, scholars of democratic persuasion – mostly Social Democrats according to party affiliation – would teach an approach to domestic and foreign politics focusing on equality and social justice, on peaceful conflict settlement, an abandonment of territorial demands and renunciation of hegemony. They either lost their positions in 1933, or were forced into exile. After 1945, these were the individuals who would come to play a decisive part in the re-establishment of the Berlin Institute.

Differences between the functional and democratic approaches surfaced most visibly in their analyses of Italian fascism and National Socialism. While not mincing words about the "browbeating" of the press and of the opposition parties in Italy, Theodor Heuss maintained that Mussolini's "personality" made him a "leader" (Heuss 1926: 97). When Heuss in 1932 published an inquiry into the German Nazi leader's political development, entitled *Hitler's Course*, a reviewer was struck by "a lack of flatly repudiating National Socialism's most ruthless attributes" (cf. Jäckel 1968: XXIV). Such lack can hardly be explained by "contemporary uncertainties" (ibid.: XXXVI). Rather, it revealed an analytical uncertainty typical of the functional approach. The democratic school, in contrast, predicted that a Nazi regime would bring "the end of the rule of law in a centralized police state" (Neumann 1973 [11932]: 109), even foreseeing that the Nazi party, "forced to let down", after its advent to power, many supporters, would "have to resort to force not just against adversaries, but against a good many followers" (Holborn 1933: 25). These, however, were rare observations. To pass the acid test, political science at the DHfP would have had to focus, first, on the gradual infringement, by established elites, of the Weimar constitution and, second, on the aggressive reactionary populism of the Nazi mass movement. The brief references just quoted indicate the achievements of which a homogeneous discipline, in the sense of a general commitment to democratic values, might have been capable. As matters stood, no adequate analytical assessment of National Socialism emerged at the DHfP.

IV

British political scientists of the inter-war period "wrote about themes and issues that still resonate today", and thereby "shaped... the ideas of the post-war makers" of the discipline. There was a continued "reluctance to embrace... theoretical and empirical methodologies." More specifically, Harold Laski's work and intellectual legacy reinforced the tendency toward "a predominance of political theory" – and, at the heart of that theory, debates about the nature of political power and the claims of the state (Kavanagh 2003: 594; Dunleavy/Kelly/Moran 2000: 4, 6; Kelly 2010: IX-XI, 20).

West German political science, initially pursued "from a Weimar perspective" (Günther 1986: 28) – which meant a determination to draw lessons from Germany's recent history – was also conceived as a highly normative enterprise. Largely devoid of empirical research and methodological reflection, it emphasized classical political theory, the institutions and decision-making processes of representative democracies, with a special focus on political parties and interest groups, and the distinction of Western political pluralism from "totalitarian rule", both of the Nazi and of the Communist variety.

In 1950, as briefly mentioned before, the DHfP was re-launched, again in an attempt to reach out to people outside the normal academic strata. Otto Suhr, who had counted among its pre-1933 instructors and was now serving as social-democratic chair of West Berlin's City Council, became the institute's first director. Subsequently, he would rise to the position of Lord Mayor. A (Research) Institute for Political Science was added to West Berlin's Free University as a joint DHfP-University enterprise a year later with United States financial support (Stammer 1960: 175, 177). But only by 1959, the DHfP itself was integrated into that university as an interdepartmental center, named after Suhr.

During 1967-69, the Otto Suhr Institute became a focal point for the movement of radical dissent, in which political science and sociology students played an influential part. LSE, too, was affected – even if less drastically – by "the troubles", as accounts were wont to refer to the explosion of student discontents (Dahrendorf 1995: 443). For a time, and to a certain extent, the sort of partial "rearrangement of research priorities" followed which David Easton had felt bound to demand from the discipline, including the construction of political alternatives, rather than "uncritically acquiesc(ing) in prevailing politics" (Easton 1969: 1058/1059, 1061).

The rest of the chapter will briefly look, on the one hand, at the contribution to British "New Left" thinking by Ralph Miliband who studied under Laski and taught at LSE until 1972 (after his death, a Ralph Miliband Program of public lectures and fellowships would be set up at LSE), and at Paul Hirst's 1990s theory of associative democracy, which built on Laski's pluralism. On the other hand, the paper will as briefly discuss Karl Dietrich Bracher's seminal work *The Disintegration of the Weimar Republic* and Ernst Fraenkel's 1964 collection *Germany and the Western Democracies*, originating, respectively, in 1955 and 1964 from the (Research) Institute of Political Science and the re-launched DHfP.

Ralph Miliband (1924-1994) fled to England from Belgium during World War II, served in the British navy and studied at LSE, where Laski became his intellectual mentor. He subsequently taught there as lecturer, was appointed a professor at Leeds University and went on to teach in Canada and the United States. In 1959, Miliband helped launch the *New Left Review* and in 1964 the *Socialist Register* as an annual "survey of movements and ideas" (Miliband 1994). His influential 1961 study, *Parliamentary Socialism*, offering a critique of the consequences of the Labour Party's approach to politics since 1900, undertook to prove that the Labour Party

> had always been 'dogmatic, not about socialism', but about a conventional interpretation of 'the parliamentary system'. This had insulated the leadership from the mass party", had "rendered them both unwilling and unable to educate and mobilise for radical purposes their own class and activist base", and had "regularly turned to the detriment of the working classes and the advantage of Conservatism (Panitch 1995; Miliband 1972: 13, 348).

Miliband went on to write *The State in Capitalist Society* (1969), where he focused on what he termed "hegemonic" processes maintaining bourgeois class rule through value-setting and fragmenting workers' class identity by a multitude of agencies in society, culture and the mass media, education and, finally, by political party machines. "Careful to acknowledge the positive features in 'bourgeois democracy', such as diversity of opinion and of freedoms", he became increasingly critical not only of the Soviet Union, but also of Cuba and China (Newman 2002: 197, 229). In *Marxism and Politics*

(1977), Miliband argued that if Marxists continued to regard politics "as an epiphenomenon" of economics, it would be impossible to construct that democracy which "he regarded as an integral part of socialism", involving "a vast extension of democratic participation in all areas of civic life" (ibid.: 233, 236).

During that same period, questions of liberal democracy and representative government certainly provided the "dominant paradigm" for British political science. As in the German case, fascism and Stalinism had "discredited a variety of alternatives to and critical views of representative democracy". However, during the last decades of the 20th century the failings of representative government – in particular, "low levels of governmental accountability" and "defective electoral and/or party systems" – became apparent. It has been judged that these decades saw "an increasingly successful challenge" to that paradigm in British political science, part of which was presaged by "notable figures such as Ralph Miliband" and other New Left thinkers (Hirst 1989, 1; Hirst 1994: 3; Kelly 2010: 25).

Projects of "'workers' control' and industrial democracy…, echoing ideas" of the early Laski and of G. D. H. Cole, also helped the concepts of pluralism and associationalism to resurface "as paths to democracy" (Kelly 2010: 27). The principal protagonist of that rediscovery was the radical political theorist Paul Hirst (1947-2003). Editing a volume of Cole's and Laski's writings in 1989, he proclaimed as its purpose to put that "important body of work back on the current agenda of political theory" (Hirst 1989: 1). Five years later, he presented what he termed a "model of associational governance in the economy and the welfare [state] sectors" (Hirst 1994: 43). Hirst carefully emphasized that he was not envisaging some "transition to an associationalist utopia", but was rather offering a "democratiz(ing)…supplement to our failing institutions…: representative mass democracy, bureaucratic state welfare and the big corporation" (ibid.: 42/43). From there he proceeded to lay the foundations of associationalist ethics, associationalist management of the economy by locally based, democratically governed firms and decentralized capital-labor bargaining, finally an associationalist system of public services through the introduction of self-governing voluntary agencies in public-private partnership.

From the outset, Hirst (1989: 2/3) had pointed out that

> English political pluralism labours under a difficulty in that it shares the word with a different, influential, and contemporary conceptual scheme… refer(ring) to a body of modern American political theory which defines democracy as a form of stable and institutionalized political competition.

In post-World War II West Germany, the experience of exile in the United States during the Nazi regime by political scientists, in particular by the influential Ernst Fraenkel (1898-1975), favoured the emergence of a "neo"-

pluralist concept largely analogous to the American model and indeed influenced by it. The approach was judged in retrospect "probably the most important product of the early stage of (West-German) political science" (Blanke et al. 1975: 76).

Expressly repudiating Laski's variety of political pluralism, and substituting totalitarianism – "the construct beyond the 'Iron Curtain' and the Wall" (Fraenkel 1968: 165) – for state monism as the principal counterpart to pluralism, the notion of "neo"-pluralism served as a perfect Cold War term. Fraenkel, who pushed it vigorously in Germany and the Western Democracies, did not mince his words in professing that neo-pluralism was "fighting – to say nothing of Hitler's shadow – the much-less faded shadow of Stalin" (ibid.: 187).

Hitler's shadow: In 1954, a Historical Section had been added to Berlin's (Research) Institute of Political Science. It came to be directed by Karl Dietrich Bracher, a 32 year-old scholar whose experience with American democracy – derived, first, from lectures during two years in a US POW camp and, subsequently, from post-doctoral studies at Harvard – had fostered his desire to come to grips with the catastrophe of Nazism (Rupp/Noetzel 1994: 18). His 800-page volume *The Disintegration of the Weimar Republic* was recognized, four years after publication, as "without question the most important study dealing with the Weimar Republic that has appeared to date" (Epstein 1959: 62) and has stood the test of time very well. Combining profound structural analysis with a formidable richness of historical detail, Bracher's book focused on the reasons for and the many strands of the "widespread movement" (ibid.) to replace democracy by dictatorship that emerged after 1919 and rapidly gained momentum during 1930-1933. Bracher explicitly stated his aim to contribute, by his analysis, to the foundations of a democratic polity (Bracher 1978 [[1]1955]: XIX).

V

Since the 1960s, the normative paradigms, both in Great Britain and in West Germany, were challenged by the onslaught of the behavioralist and systems theory approaches which "modern" American political science had developed. If at LSE, the Department of Politics (now labeled Government Department) continued to attract a "set of outstanding individual scholars", their common denominator would, however, remain "the absence of empirical political science" (Dahrendorf 1995: 415).

In his 1957 LSE doctoral thesis, Bernard Crick (later Sir Bernard Crick, 1929-2008) incisively argued that "the construction of a democratic order... required a historical study of politics rather than the scientism of the behavioralists" (Grant 2010: 35). Published two years later, Crick's *American Science of Politics* "became a very influential book" (ibid.: 34); the work's dictum "Politics is normally the application of experience to the creative conciliation of differing interests" (Crick 1959: 221) may be considered thoroughly in the spirit of British political studies. Another three years later, in a chapter of his even more renowned volume In *Defence of Politics*, Crick once again rejected any major role of scientism for the discipline (Crick 2rev1964: ch. 5). Appointed a lecturer at LSE and subsequently Professor of Political Theory at Sheffield University, Crick was knighted in 2002 for "services to citizenship in [secondary] schools", where his efforts had led to the establishment of compulsory citizenship classes.

To some extent, Crick's attitude would seem to mirror the overall response of the British discipline to the "American challenge": Acceptance of the overseas model has been "reluctant"; integration of American approaches happened in "homeopathic doses"; and normative political theory has retained a considerably stronger position (Grant 2010: 33, 163, 167).

In (West) Germany, the discipline's "Americanization", commencing by the mid-1960s, initially progressed more rapidly than in Great Britain. However, the "strengthening of behaviourist approaches was interrupted" by the leftist protest movement of the late 60s (Beyme 1982: 95). Even then, younger scholars continued to assimilate American methodological concepts, particularly with regard to policy analysis (ibid.: 96, 98). Since the 1980s, normative theories have been on the retreat and policy studies on the advance. As a result, German political science impresses the observer as more fragmented today than its British counterpart.

References

Beveridge, Lord (1952): "Introduction", in: *Beatrice Webb's Diaries*, ed. Margaret Cole, London: Longmans, Green, pp. V-XVIII
Beyme, Klaus von (1982): "Modern Schools of Politics: Western Germany", *Government & Opposition* Vol. 17 (1982), pp. 94-107
Blanke, Bernhard/Jürgens, Ulrich/Kastendiek, Hans (1975): *Kritik der politischen Wissenschaft*, Vol. 1, Frankfurt/New York: Campus
Bracher, Karl Dietrich (1978 [11955]: *Die Auflösung der Weimarer Republik*, Droste: Düsseldorf/Königstein: Athenäum.
Crick, Bernard (1959): *The American Science of Politics. Its Origins and Conditions*, London: Routledge & Kegan Paul
Crick, Bernard ([2rev]1964 [[1]1962]: *In Defence of Politics*, Harmondsworth: Penguin Books
Dahrendorf, Ralf (1995): *LSE. A History of the London School of Economics and Political Science*, 1895-1995, Oxford/New York: Oxford University Press

Deane, Harold A. (1955): *The Political Ideas of Harold J. Laski*, New York: Columbia University Press

Dewey, John (1954): *The Public and its Problems*, Denver: Alan Swallow.

Döring, Herbert (1975): *Der Weimarer Kreis*, Meisenheim: Hain

Dunleavy, Patrick/Kelly, P. J./Moran, Michael (2000): "Characterizing the Development of British Political Science", in: id. (eds.): *British Political Science: 50 Years of Political Studies*, Oxford: Blackwell, 3-9

Easton, David (1969): "The New Revolution in Political Science", *American Political Science Review* Vol. LXIII, pp. 1051-1061

Epstein, Klaus (1959): „Review" of Karl Dietrich Bracher: Die Auflösung der Weimarer Republik, *Journal of Modern History* Vol. 31, pp.62-63

Faulenbach, Bernd (1980): *Ideologie des deutschen Weges*, Munich.

Fraenkel, Ernst (1968): Deutschland und die westlichen Demokratien, Stuttgart: Kohlhammer

Grant, Wyn (2010): *The Development of a Discipline. The History of the Political Studies Association*, Chichester: Wiley-Blackwell

Grant, Wyn (2013): *Personal communication*

Griffith, Thomas H. (1933): *Politischer Pluralismus in der zeitgenössischen Philosophie Englands, Dissertation*, University of Giessen

Günther, Klaus (1986): „Politikwissenschaft in der Bundesrepublik und die jüngste deutsche Geschichte", in: Klaus von Beyme (ed.): *Politikwissenschaft in der Bundesrepublik*, PVS-Sonderheft 17, Opladen: Westdeutscher Verlag, 27-40

Heslep, Robert D. (1968): "Graham Wallas and the Great Society", *Educational Theory* 18, 151-163

Heuss, Theodor (1921): „Denkschrift zur Errichtung einer Deutschen Hochschule für Politik", in: *Politische Bildung. Wille – Wesen – Ziel – Weg*, Berlin: Deutsche Verlagsgesellschaft für Politik und Geschichte, pp. 33-37.

Heuss, Theodor (1926): *Staat und Volk*, Berlin: Deutsche Buch-Gemeinschaft

Hirst, Paul (1989): "Introduction", in: id. (ed.): *The Pluralist Theory of the State. Selected Writings by G. D. H. Cole, J. N. Figgis, and H. J. Laski*, London: Routledge, pp. 1-47

Hirst, Paul (1994): *Associative Democracy*, Cambridge: Polity Press

Holborn, Hajo (1933): *Weimarer Reichsverfassung und Freiheit der Wissenschaft*, Leipzig: Meiner

Jäckel, Eberhard (1968): „Einleitung", in: Theodor Heuss: *Hitlers Weg*, new ed. [11932], Tübingen: Wunderlich, pp. XI-XLIV

Jäckh, Ernst (1921):„Rede", in: *Politische Bildung. Wille – Wesen – Ziel – Weg*. Berlin: Deutsche Verlagsgesellschaft für Politik und Geschichte, p. 31.

Jäckh, Ernst (1952): „Die ‚alte' Hochschule für Politik", in: id./Suhr, Otto: *Geschichte der Deutschen Hochschule für Politik*, Berlin: Gebr. Weiss, pp. 5-32.

Jäckh, Ernst (1960): *Weltsaat*, Stuttgart: Deutsche Verlagsanstalt.

Kavanagh, Dennis (2003): "British Political Science in the Inter-War Years: The Emergence of the Founding Fathers", *British Journal of Politics & International Relations* 5, 594-613

Kelly, Paul (2010): *British Political Theory in the Twentieth Century*, Chichester: Wiley-Blackwell

Kramnick, Isaac/Sheerman, Barry (1993): *Harold Laski. A Life on the Left*, New York: Penguin

Laski, Harold J. (1919): *Authority in the Modern State*, New Haven: Yale University Press

Laski, Harold J. (1925): *A Grammar of Politics* (reprint 1948), London: George Allen/Unwin

Miliband, Ralph (1972, 11961): *Parliamentary Socialism*, London: Merlin Press

Miliband, Ralph (1994): "Thirty Years of the Socialist Register", *www.marxists. org/archive/miliband/1994/xx/30socreg.htm*

Neumann, Sigmund (1973, 11932): *Die Parteien der Weimarer Republik*, Stuttgart: Kohlhammer.

Newman, Michael (2002): *Ralph Miliband and the Politics of the New Left*, London: Merlin Press.

Panitch, Leo (1995): "Ralph Miliband, Socialist Intellectual, 1924-1994", *www. marxists.org/archive/Miliband/biog/panitch.htm*

Spahn, Martin (1922/23):"Vorspann", in: Politisches Kolleg, Hochschule für nationale Politik, *Vorlesungsverzeichnis 1922/23*, Berlin, p. 3

Struve, Walter (1973): *Elites Against Democracy. Leadership Ideals in Bourgeois Political Thought in Germany*, 1890-1933, Princeton: Princeton University Press.

Webb, Sidney (1920): "Introduction", in: *Fabian Essays*, ed. G. B. Shaw, London: Allen and Unwin, pp. XV-XXVII.

Did Ernst Jaeckh and Arnold Wolfers, leading figures of the Weimar Republic's Berlin Political Studies Institute, who emigrated to the United States after Hitler came to power, assume any significance for the establishment of the International-al Relations discipline in that country? Certainly, they pale in comparison to Hans Morgenthau, John Herz, or Karl Deutsch. However, what may be learnt from looking at their cases is that (1) Wolfers' initial infatuation with Nazism, which he brought to the United States, did not preclude him from obtaining a prestigious position at Yale; (2) that Wolfers symbolized to an extraordinary ex-tent the close ties of the discipline with American political and military agencies; (3) that Jaeckh likewise knew how to sell himself to political players, dissembling on his attempts to collaborate with the Nazis and, in his case, coloring his life-long turkophile narratives according to the perceived exigencies of changing constellations. The following chapter first appeared in a collection on Emigré Scholars and the Genesis of International Relations, edited in 2014 by Felix Rösch (Coventry).

From the Berlin Political Studies Institute to Columbia and Yale: Ernst Jaeckh and Arnold Wolfers

I

During the Weimar Republic, the paths of German-born Ernst Jaeckh (1875-1959) and Swiss-born Arnold Wolfers (1892-1968) crossed in Berlin, where both came to share an institutional affiliation with the German Political Stud-ies Institute (*Deutsche Hochschule für Politik*, DHfP). Jaeckh served as DHfP Chair, subsequently President (1920-33). Wolfers, having joined the Institute as lecturer in 1925, was appointed studies supervisor (1927-30), eventually DHfP Director under Jaeckh (1930-33).

After the Dawes Plan had been signed in 1924 and the role of reparations agent devolved on the United States, Jaeckh astutely judged that growing economic involvement would trigger American political interest in Weimar Germany. He was encouraged by Wolfers, who returned from a 1925 trip to the U. S. convinced that the country's political and military "supremacy" based on economic strength would be "merely a matter of time" (Wolfers 1925: 14, 17). Jaeckh and Wolfers successfully targeted the Rockefeller Foundation and the Carnegie Endowment for International Peace as "pro-spective financial supporters" (Korenblat 2008: 108): From 1926, both foun-dations became involved in subsidizing the *Hochschule* – its archives, its library, its publications, its short-lived (1932) research division. A first Carnegie Chair – to be awarded on a yearly basis, or to be used for paying visiting lecturers -was established in 1927, another (held by Hajo Holborn) in 1931.

On a second level, that of international intellectual cooperation, Jaeckh and Wolfers went on successive American lecture tours, spoke at Britain's Royal Institute of International Affairs (Chatham House), at the Geneva Institute of International Relations, had their presentations on the "New Germany" published as books (Jaeckh) or in journals such as *International Affairs* (Wolfers). Unwittingly, they prepared the ground for careers in exile, into which both headed after the Nazis had come to power. Jaeckh went to London, later (1940) proceeding to the United States. Wolfers immediately went to the U. S.

However, unlike other scholars forced into exile – such as Hannah Arendt, Ernst Fraenkel, George W. F. Hallgarten, John H. Herz, Hajo Holborn, Karl Löwenstein, Hans J. Morgenthau, Franz Leopold Neumann -, Jaeckh and Wolfers initially misjudged Nazism, even during 1933, as merely a 'more determined' variety of national community-building, a 'more vigorous' brand of revisionism ('revision' referring, of course, to the removal of the constraints imposed on Germany by the Versailles Peace Treaty). Continuing to defend, during 1931/32, the increasingly authoritarian policies pursued by Hindenburg and his entourage as well as by Brüning's and Papen's Presidential cabinets, both consistently misread the infringement, by established elites, of the Weimar constitution and the Nazi mass movement's aggressive reactionary populism.

By mid-1933, John Wheeler-Bennett – a member of the Royal Institute of International Affairs, who would later write *The Nemesis of Power*, a highly acclaimed study on the German Army's role in the Weimar Republic – noted that Jaeckh seemed "manoeuvering, or being manoeuvered, into the post of an intellectual ambassador of the new regime" (Sickle 1933: 2). In Wolfers' case, it took some 60 years until one of his former American students would admit that, during the 1930s, even while already ensconced at Yale, Wolfers had for a time been "attracted to Hitler for his anticommunism and pan-European rhetoric" (Stuart 1994: 5).

II

During the Great War, the political journalist Jaeckh had collaborated with Friedrich Naumann in promoting German war aims. Naumann – a publicist and politician who became famous in 1915 when he circulated his ideas on a "fourth world empire" *Mitteleuropa* (Central Europe) to be shaped by Germany – had earlier supported a "democratic imperialism" promoting domestic social reforms to secure a more solid foundation for overseas expansion (Naumann 1900). Jaeckh was not satisfied with supporting Naumann's design of a Central Europe "unified under German leadership... against England and America on one, against Russia on the other side" (Fischer 1969: 746). Driven by inflated war-time expectations, he had proclaimed a "Greater Central Europe" – Germany, Austria-Hungary, Turkey, Bulgaria, Romania, and Greece – to be led "organically", "without despotism", by the German Empire, complementing Germany's "seaward orientation, especially toward a future 'Middle Africa'" (Jaeckh 1916: 6, 11, 17). The extent to which conceptual pathology was rampant in Germany during 1914-18 may be indicated by the fact that 'liberal-imperialist' programs like Jaeckh's were considered 'moderate', because they renounced formal annexations, focused on Eastern rather than Western Europe, and lacked a repressive domestic element.

For his efforts, Jaeckh had been awarded a chair in 1916 at the Institute of Oriental Languages (*Orientalisches Seminar*) established by Bismarck as a facility for training recruits to the Foreign Service. Incidentally, George F. Kennan would later emerge as that Institute's most renowned student: Kennan took his Russian language examination in 1930 and went on to study Russian history for another year at the University of Berlin under Otto Hoetzsch and Karl Stählin (Kennan 1983: 31/32; on Hoetzsch, who also taught at the DHfP, see Eisfeld 1991: 45, 52/53).

Since 1908, Jaeckh had put his bets on "the New Turkey's allegedly rising crescent", promoting a "sense of German proprietorship in an Anatolian place in the sun" (Anderson 2007: 107). He had been publishing works such as *Der aufsteigende Halbmond* (1908, Engl. rev. ed. *The Rising Crescent* 1944) or *Deutschland im Orient nach dem Balkankrieg* (*Germany in the Near East after the Balkan War,* 1913), and had established in 1914 the German-Turkish Association, chaired by Karl Helfferich (*Deutsche Bank*). Skilfully dissembling, as will be demonstrated below, his past in more ways than one, he would later label his ambitions "German-Turkish 'Truman politics'... against Russia's imperialism" (Jaeckh 1954: 209).

Jaeckh did not stop at extolling the virtues of the "New Turkey". Fascinated by the perspective of transforming the "ailing" multi-ethnic Ottoman Empire into a strong nation state, he supported the Young Turk government's "Turkification" project that involved purging the Armenian minority from the population (on the program, see Dabag 2002: 36/37, 39). When increasingly frequent accounts of systematic Turkish atrocities against the Armenians started arriving in Germany, Jaeckh – as executive secretary of the German-Turkish Association – strongly tried to prevent dissemination of reports on the genocide.

At this point, it should be recalled that Imperial Germany had itself committed genocide in German South-West Africa (today Namibia) just a decade earlier by killing, or allowing to perish from thirst in the sealed-off desert and from exhaustion and disease in concentration camps, over 50,000 members of the Herero and Nama tribes (Drechsler 1980; Hull 2005). When the Social Democrats, the Catholic Center party, and national minorities' parties had rejected a supplementary military budget, Chancellor von Bülow had dissolved the Reichstag and called the infamous 1907 "Hottentot" elections, in which the Social Democrats had lost half their seats.

In 1916, Jaeckh requested the German Foreign Office to bar Johannes Lepsius, chair of the German-Armenian Association, from a lecture tour to Switzerland. Subsequently, he proposed that military censorship should prohibit any domestic lectures on the Turkish massacres. Both measures were rejected as inexpedient by the Foreign Office (Goltz 2002: 365/366; also Kloosterhuis 1994, Vol. 1: 255; Vol. 2: 660, 661 n. 7/8). However, they testified to an amoral streak in the man that would surface again.

Before his death in 1919, Naumann had suggested establishing a center of political education. He had even started a "civics school" for the liberal Progressive People's Party *(Fortschrittliche Volkspartei*, FVP) which, after the 1918 revolution, was reorganized into the German Democratic Party *(Deutsche Demokratische Partei*, DDP). When Jaeckh took over from Naumann, he endeavoured to put the venture on a broader, *überparteilich* (non-partisan) basis: The institute was to provide "a focal point around which to crystallize a new Germany and, thereby, a new Europe possessed by a new spirit (albeit not the pointless, brutal 'spirit' of Versailles" (Jaeckh 1921: 31). Another of Naumann's followers equally did not mince his words. Theodor Heuss, the future institute's first studies supervisor (much later, of course, also the German Federal Republic's first president) contended that German politics, "forced into a system of humiliations by external force and through its own fault", knew "but *one* issue: the struggle for national liberation" (Heuss 1921: 33/34). To that aim, the DHfP had to contribute by instruction and example.

From post-World War II 'reprints' of his earlier speech (Jaeckh 1952: 14: id. 1960: 87/88), Jaeckh would regularly omit the part about "the pointless, brutal 'spirit' of Versailles". At the time, however, the revisionist impulse was unmistakable. The necessary funds were initially provided, first and foremost, by Prussia and the *Reich*, supplemented by grants from a few industrialists (Bosch, Siemens). The reform-minded Prussian Minister of Education, Carl Heinrich Becker (like Jaeckh, an earlier promoter of a German-Turkish "union of interests"), echoed Jaeckh and Heuss: Fostering political understanding should be "deliberately" employed "to strengthen Germany domestically and to come to terms with other peoples externally" (Becker 1919: 13).

For the institute's founders and sponsors, the purpose of political science consisted in aiding German aspirations to recapture the country's pre-war position of power on the continent, refusing to acknowledge the defeat of 1918.

Even where Jaeckh ostensibly invoked the "new" spirit of a "new" Europe, he merely took into account the fundamentally changed European environment affecting Germany's traditional aim of continental hegemony. His position was evidenced by his, and Heuss', rejection of the Pan-European proposals submitted by French Foreign Minister Aristide Briand (Heuss 1929: 117; Jaeckh 1932a: 46).

III

Reacting to the 1918 revolution, the literary and art historian Arthur Moeller van den Bruck – who would write the notorious pamphlet *The Third Reich* before committing suicide in 1925 – had gathered around himself a "revolutionary-conservative" circle proclaiming the "politicization of the nation" under mass-based authoritarian (rather than traditional monarchical) leadership. When the Versailles Treaty was signed in June, 1919, the circle assumed the name June Club to express its protest.

Basically, "politicizing the nation" was not too different from what Jaeckh and his more moderate faction had in mind. For the June club, however, the revision of Versailles had to commence "by the revision of Weimar" (Mariaux 1932: 83): Domestically no less than externally, every main result of the Great War was to be undone. Once again, political science would have to contribute: Like Jaeckh and his collaborators, the revolutionary-conservative group began planning for a school of politics. A week after the DHfP had been inaugurated on October 24, 1920, the June Club established its Political College (*Politisches Kolleg*), appealing to a "militant and manly community" of students "unwilling to let the fatherland perish by the hands of inadequate leaders and external enemies" (Politisches Kolleg 1922/23: 3). Financial support was provided by heavy industry through Alfred Hugenberg.

When the rabidly nationalist German National People's Party (*Deutschnationale Volkspartei*, DNVP) in 1927 temporarily joined a governmental coalition – before its final, fatal radicalization unter Hugenberg's leadership that would ally it with the Nazis (Beck 2008) –, the *Hochschule* and the *Kolleg* concluded a formal cooperation agreement. The *Arbeitsgemeinschaft* was continued, even enlarged, on an informal basis from 1930, and the revolutionary-conservative program increasingly took hold at the DHfP. The individual who, according to June Club associate Heinz Brauweiler (Brauweiler 1932: 1), "energetically and successfully" pressed for an arrangement that favored the *Kolleg*'s cause, was Arnold Wolfers.

IV

When Wolfers joined the DHfP faculty in 1925, he was already on his way of very rapidly turning from a religious socialist into a "self-styled 'Tory-Liberal'" (Winks 1987: 40). Within a few years, he would denounce "an extreme form of democratic constitution" as the "inherent weakness" of the Weimar Republic (Wolfers 1932: 758). Having earned his LLD from Zurich University in 1917, Wolfers had received his PhD from Giessen University a year before involving himself with the Berlin institute. In his dissertation, entitled *The Establishment of Capitalist Hegemony in Occidental Society*, he emphasized the effectiveness of "plutocratic power in politics and society" (Wolfers 1924: 163). Subsequently, he underwent his 'Damascus experience':

A four months-trip to the United States, already mentioned at this chapter's outset, made him conclude that "a capitalist economy far surpassing European dimensions" might co-exist with "the vibrant reality... of a middle class democracy" that did not exclude workers "from any cultural or spiritual possessions" (Wolfers 1925: 4/5). Wolfers contended that middle class reality and middle class ideal provided the basis for a "consciousness of unity under the Stars and Stripes" (ibid.: 10, 13) that enabled the United States to project economic, political, and military pressure into the international arena. American supremacy would therefore be "merely a matter of time", and Wolfers left no doubt that he considered such strength exemplary for overcoming German "divisiveness and fragmentation" (ibid.: 14, 17).

The diagnosis bore a striking resemblance to the picture painted by a study which Jaeckh published four years later: a unified society under strong leadership, capable in international relations of what Jaeckh labeled "pacifist imperialism". In even stronger terms than Wolfers, Jaeckh described the United States as a "society of equal opportunities", "not burdened" by the conflict between capital and labor, whose global policies were directed by "a small group", an "actual leading elite", conscious of a "joint ideology". Regarding the character of these policies, Jaeckh again echoed Wolfers (Jaeckh 1929: 13, 31, 105): "Economic or political pressure, taking advantage of economic or political chances, implying a pacifist policy of conquest – those were, from the outset, the method and the principles of American imperialism."

Domestically geared to American society, internationally allied with the United States – such was Jaeckh's recipe for German resurgence, phrased with an emphasis typical of the man (ibid.: 17, 105): "The 'American heart of the world' and the 'German heart of Europe' – they beat at the same pace... The time has arrived when Carl Schurz' words will be fulfilled: 'America's influence in Europe will be based on Germany, and Germany's position in the world will essentially rest on America's success.'"

As late as 1932, Jaeckh would identify "Germany's biological right to exist" with the "biological changeability" (curious term) "of the Versailles Treaty" (Jaeckh 1932b: 791). During 1931/32, and into 1933, Jaeckh continued to defend, in response to sceptical British and American interrogators, the increasingly authoritarian policies pursued by Hindenburg and his entourage, by Brüning's and Papen's Presidential administrations. Hindenburg was sized up by Jaeckh as "the German Washington: 'first in war, first in peace'"; he and his State Secretary Otto Meissner, "equally experienced and trustworthy", would continue "safeguarding the constitution". Brüning was judged by Jaeckh "the synthesis of thinking-action known only in the old Greek philosophers", Papen " 'le chevalier sans peur et sans reproche' " – "reactionary? No – if 'reactionary' means essaying an unconstitutional policy or trying to turn backward the wheel of evolution" (Jaeckh 1931c; 1932c: 2; 1933a: 10, 11, 20). Seriously flawed assumptions and effusive personal praise added up to gross political misjudgements. Attempting to reach an accommodation even with Nazism could, as a result, seem merely one more small step.

Wolfers likewise consistently misread the authoritarian and racist threat to the Weimar Republic. The reasons that made him join, between 1925 and 1930, the camp of "constructive" (his term) revisionists are difficult to determine. Up to the autumn of 1932, Wolfers would echo Jaeckh to the effect that constitutional "reforms" contemplated by Hindenburg ("a pillar of democracy") and the Papen government were "moderate". He would also insist that the danger of "dictatorship by one party [had] been taken from Germany" and that, finally, the mass-based Nazi party offered "a safeguard against social reaction", even providing a "force making for democracy" that was ever more "likely to come to the fore" (Wolfers 1932: 769, 771).

Subsequent to January, 1933, Wolfers persisted in the same sort of self-deception about Nazism which would be exhibited by Jaeckh. Because of a Jewish strain in his family, the Nazi regime put him on the list of undesirables. In late April, 1933, he left for Yale, where he had been offered the position of Visiting Professor of International Relations for the coming academic year. Undauntedly, Wolfers went on to inform American audiences that "Hitler [had] the very highest esteem for what he calls 'European culture' to defend against the threat of 'Asiatic bolshevism' " (Wolfers 1933: 188).

V

Looking back, from the distance of a decade, on the destruction of the Weimar Republic and the liquidation of the Berlin Political Studies Institute, Ernst Jaeckh would present himself , in a book impressively titled *The War for Man's Soul*, as a cool, calm adversary of the Nazis, a shrewd, unfazed judge of men and events. Hindenburg, State Secretary Meissner, former *Reichsbank* President Hjalmar Schacht, above all Papen were now dubbed "pathetically deceived deceivers", "short-sighted nationalists", "narrow-minded reactionaries". Goebbels became the "devil" whom he, Jaeckh, had been able to "dupe" by deciding to "fight" over the *Hochschule für Politik* (Jaeckh 1943: 66 ss., 72 ss., 107/108):

> "For once, this Machiavelli, nay Mephistopheles of the Hitlerites was not to have his way by threats and brute force. I wanted him to acknowledge rights and laws."

Reality, in several ways (as evidenced by earlier quotes from Jaeckh's talks), had been different from his assertions. By 1943, Jaeckh would contend that, after the rigged elections of March 5, 1933, he had decided to "leave Germany for good", because now "terror and lawlessness would deluge the country" (ibid.: 107). When addressing, on March 27, the participants of a DHfP course for Prussian civil servants, he had sounded very different (Jaeckh 1933b: 401):

> "Three major, even historically decisive dates have intervened between the present and the last course: January 30, March 5, March 21. In turn, they signify: the legal transition of governmental power to a revolutionary movement; the seizure of that power by the national revolution; the legitimization of that revolution by the nation as embodied in the Reichstag."

Attempting to convince the regime that it might benefit from the *Hochschule* if it would only forgo complete Nazification (viz. putting Goebbels' Propaganda Ministry in charge), Jaeckh – according to Rockefeller Foundation officer John Van Sickle – displayed an "extraordinary capacity of adaptation" (Sickle 1933: 2). The Berlin Institute could be used, he wrote Prussian Minister of Education Bernhard Rust, as a "unique" instrument "to speak out abroad in favour of German revision politics" (Jaeckh 1933d: 411). As Jaeckh impressed on Hitler's aide Hans Heinrich Lammers, new chief of the Reich Chancellery, he had "access to the whole British press, actually to any kind of conference in London, Oxford, or Cambridge" (Jaeckh 1933c: 37). Lammers arranged a meeting between Hitler and Jaeckh on April 1, 1933. A decade later, Jaeckh would melodramatically embellish his report on the encounter, from disarmingly greeting "with a Swabian 'Grüß Gott!'" the guards hollering 'Heil Hitler!', to his early prediction of the *Führer*'s doom (Jaeckh 1943: 97). The meeting itself was inconclusive. Hitler simply referred Jaeckh to Goebbels for further discussing the matter of the DHfP's intended transfer to the auspices of the Propaganda Ministry.

The transfer, however, was already definite. Goebbels had carried the day against Rust. On April 16, Jaeckh advised Lammers of his resignation from the office of President of the Political Studies Institute. Later, Jaeckh would publish two versions of his resignation letter – one in the United States (1943), another in Germany (1952). Both were severely distorted. The letter's first printed version (Jaeckh 1943: 290/291) was terse and to the point. Consisting of six sentences, one mere paragraph, it read impressive, because it *omitted* four fifths of the original text. The second published version (Jaeckh 1952: 20/21) was morally questionable to a much greater extent, *adding* a further paragraph *that had never been included in the resignation letter*. Part, but merely part, came from an address which Jaeckh had given *six weeks later – not in Germany, but in London* (Jaeckh 1933f: 3):

"That the Hochschule is now taken over by the state has meant (among other things) the application of the new regulations for civil servants, including the 'Arian Paragraphs' [,] to my Hochschule. In other words, it would have meant dismissing those of my tried and valued friends and fellow[-]workers who came under those regulations. I could not bring myself to do that, and therefore resigned."

The remaining sentences, as published in 1952, had been *completely fabricated* by Jaeckh:

"You know yourself that and how I have made no secret of my view that the present persecution of Jews, which I condemn, is an injustice as un-German as it is inhuman. All my life, I have sided with those who were unjustly oppressed and persecuted. To me, this is a must."

On April 1, 1933, when Jaeckh was received by Hitler, the regime had organized the first public boycott against Jewish stores. To have, supposedly, protested that ominous act with a noble, at the time already exceptional statement must have seemed an attractive idea to Jäckh after World War II.

His actual letter to Lammers (Jäckh 1933e: 90/91) cannot be reproduced here in full (for the complete text, see Eisfeld 1991: 101/102). The main reason for Jäckh's later distortions was that it certainly did not reveal the writer's decision "to leave Germany for good". Jaeckh was merely laying out new activities for himself. After informing Lammers about his resignation from the office of DHfP President, he continued:

"Regardless whether Germany may be termed a First, Second, or Third Reich, I remain resolved to serve our common mother country and the German nation… I hope I may go on counting on your approving and favorable support, whether in heading the Rockefeller Institute of Political Research, in my informational activities abroad, or in some other connection."

Even after his strategy of accommodation had failed, Jaeckh, undaunted, would embark on a new course – the establishment of a Research Institute of International Relations, financed by the Rockefeller Foundation, its trustees and staff carefully parceled out between figures of "liberal" and "national(-socialist)" affiliation. Only when those efforts, too, came to nothing (for details, see Eisfeld 1996: 38/39), Jaeckh would liquidate the *Hochschule* and go into exile. The liquidation was only completed by early 1934, when Jaeckh had already established himself in Great Britain. During that period, he "held his ground" with the regime, insuring that government contributions which had earlier been negotiated were fully paid, and that deposed DHfP scholars received "fair compensation" (Korenblat 1978: 335). His persistence particularly benefited those who, in difficult circumstances, either remained in Germany, like Theodor Heuss, or went into exile, like Sigmund Neumann.

VI

Subsequent to the March 5 Reichstag elections, Friedrich Wilhelm von Prittwitz und Gaffron resigned his position as ambassador in Washington. He would remain the sole high-ranking German civil servant to quit the diplomatic service after Hitler had come to power. In this, he displayed better judgment and more moral fiber than Arnold Wolfers, of whom the German Embassy cabled to Berlin on February 27, 1934 that he had "been active as a speaker for the New Germany in a most vigorous manner...during the last months... On February 3, for instance, he gave a talk to the 'Foreign Policy Association' in New York, successfully defending the *Reich* Government's foreign policy" (Deutsche Botschaft Washington 1934).

Wolfers not only made a case for the Nazi regime's attempt "to invoke the positive soldierly virtues – frugality, discipline, and authority... enlist[ing] the wartime spirit of camaraderie and unity... to rebuild Germany along these principles" (Murray 1934). He also displayed astonishingly wishful thinking when he offered his guess that it might "become the greatest ambition of European dictatorships to prove that they are better able than their democratic predecessors, by reason of their independence of parliamentary pressure, to give peace to Europe and the world" (Wolfers 1933).

His errors of judgment before and after January 30, 1933 did not preclude Wolfers from being appointed, by mid-1935, professor of international relations and (until 1949, when he was elevated to a Sterling professorship) master of the prestigious Pierson College, one of Yale's – at the time – seven Residential Colleges. He maintained his attitude of qualified benevolence to Nazi Germany even after that country had unleashed World War II. In *Britain and France Between Two Wars*, "the only real book he wrote during his American career" (Martin 1994: 11), Wolfers – again misreading the aims and character of Hitler's war – argued for an "agreement" between Britain, France, Germany, and Italy "on the extent of their respective power and position in the East and West... and in the Mediterranean" (Wolfers 1940: 390).

A former First Lieutenant in the Swiss army, Wolfers – in contrast to other exiled social scientists – not merely advised the State Department and the Office of Strategic Services, but also (from 1942) the School of Military Government, (from 1947) the National War College, and (from 1960) the Institute of Defense Analyses (Strauss/Röder 1983: 1259). Becoming extremely well connected in the inner workings of American political and military agencies, he served as a "conduit" to the intelligence community, "often steer[ing] appropriate young men into intelligence work", "a disproportionate number" of whom "came from Pierson College" (Winks 1987: 36 ss., 40/41, 241).

In 1943, while on the Board of Economic Warfare, Paul Nitze – together with Boston Representative Christian Herter – founded the School of Advanced International Studies in Washington (SAIS, today named in Nitze's honor), which became part of John Hopkins University in 1950, as a think tank for debate on foreign and security policy issues. By 1957, Nitze – having meanwhile served as Director of Policy Planning in the State Department – concluded that SAIS needed an affiliated Foreign Policy Research Center. Wolfers became the Center's first director from 1957 to 1965. "Tend[ing] to question the 'isms' and certainties popular in the academia of the days", he brought "a wind of fresh air to what had been a fairly stodgy and opinionated group" (Nitze 1994: VI).

Nitze's appraisal confirms the judgment that Wolfers' influence did not derive from what he wrote. "His written output was remarkably small…, [his 1962 collection] *Discord and Collaboration: Essays on International Politics*, more valuable though it is [than *Britain and France Between Two Wars*], being an assemblage of the again quite limited work he published in journals" (Martin 1994: 11). Wolfers excelled as a discussion leader, a communicator and mediator, interested in "always relating theory to practice" (Szabo 1994: 240). At Yale, he "stood at the center of a group of faculty…, referred to by those outside their charmed circle as 'the State Department' ", which launched a weekly faculty seminar "Where Is the World Going?", at which "various State Department issues were discussed". From this seminar Wolfers "developed study groups to tackle problems sent up from the State Department" (Winks 1987: 41), thereby exerting "a remarkable influence on a body of students who entered the… practice of diplomacy" (Martin 1994: 12).

In the debate between realist and idealist schools of thought in international relations theory, Wolfers has been dubbed a "reluctant realist" (Stuart/Szabo 1994: 1). But the gist of his position is encapsulated in a quote from his period as director of the Foreign Policy Research Center:

> "It is no accident that the Center has been labelled 'realistic', and has been criticized for an alleged 'power political' viewpoint, not merely in matters of military policy, where this would be hard to avoid, but also in its treatment of problems

connected with the UN, disarmament, or economic aid where the tendency is toward an idealistic or even an utopian approach" (cited by Szabo 1994: 240).

Not by accident, Roger Hilsman, one his former students, was still enthusiastic about counterinsurgency as a major part of the U.S. commitment to Vietnam when, in 1965, he co-edited a volume of essays in honor of Wolfers. In the chapter, Hilsman put forth his 'enlightened' arguments against "over-militarizing", propagating instead a combination "of military [i. e. Special Forces] operations, police efforts, and rural development" (Hilsman 1995: 195). Hilsman's chapter was a reprint; it had originally been published under the title: "Plea for 'Realism' in Southeast Asia".

Even if, to some extent, "refus[ing] to subscribe to any single approach" (Szabo 1994: 241), even if, again to a certain extent, "allow[ing] for the incorporation of moral standards into judgments about the behavior of states" (Stuart 1994: 5), Wolfers made rather minimalistic concessions to non-realist approaches, as testified by his following statement: "Even now survival is not always at stake. Even now there is freedom of choice between more or less moderation, more or less concern for the interests of others,... more or less respect for justice" (Wolfers/Martin 1956: 251). That these words should *ex post* have been elevated to the philosophical heights of a "vision of moral law" (Stuart 1995: 5), is a telling comment both on Wolfers and on the state of international relations theory.

Conservative, confident and cautious, married to a Swiss diplomat's daughter, as the master of Yale's Pierson College a host with style to significant public figures, Arnold Wolfers easily bridged the gap between academe and policy planning. In his ways of advising and defending U.S. Cold War policies, he – like many other intellectuals – adhered to established wisdoms, "not doubting for a moment the validity of [his] right to serve, the quality of [his] experience" (Halberstam 1992: 43). It may safely be said that publicly voicing dissent on America's Vietnam strategy, as Hans J. Morgenthau did, to the extent of getting himself dismissed as a consultant to the Department of State, would have been strange to Arnold Wolfers.

VII

"National tactics need to embark upon the road of a new international law", Jaeckh had written before the Nazis' advent to power. "The task of strategy and tactics consists in cultivating that embryonic law, developing it into an authentic new order" (Jäckh 1932a: 37). Hoping to obtain Germany's admission to the newly-formed League of Nations, Jaeckh had early on been involved in founding (by late 1918) a German League of Nations Union. He could lay claim to having, both nationally and internationally, recommended to German governments a consistent League of Nations policy aimed at securing revision of the Versailles Treaty, and including the perspective of German-Austrian union (Jaeckh 1927: 81/82, 97 ss.).

After Jaeckh had emigrated to London in 1933, he was appointed international director of the New Commonwealth Society, established a year earlier by David Davies (Lord Davies), millionaire and long-time Liberal MP, who had endowed the United Kingdom's first Chair in International Politics at the University College of Wales in 1919. The Society advocated providing the League of Nations with a police force to maintain international law. Winston Churchill, at the time out of political office, served as its president.

Obtaining renewed financial support from the Rockefeller Foundation, Jaeckh managed to enlarge the organization into an international venture that eventually included numerous national sections (Mogk 1974). His position and travels allowed Jaeckh to re-establish the sort of political contacts which he had been assiduously cultivating in Germany, including "his credentials as an expert and 'man to see' on Turkish affairs" (Korenblat 2008: 102). Jäckh seems to have succeeded in impressing that role, to a certain extent, on the British Foreign Office, even if his later overly pro-Turkish judgments on that country's role before and during World War II (Jäckh 1960: 221 ss.) should be taken with a large dose of salt.

After a brief stint with the Ministry of Information, created in 1939 after the United Kingdom had declared war on Germany (it would inspire George Orwell's "Ministry of Truth"), a Carnegie Fellowship permitted Jaeckh in 1940 to join the Columbia University faculty, first as Visiting Professor of International Relations. In a permanent position as Professor of Public Law and Government at Columbia, he committed himself to assist in establishing the university's Middle East Institute. In 1949, was among the founders, with Turkish U.N. Representative Selim Sarper (a Kemalist politician who had studied in Berlin), of the American Turkish Society, modeled on the 1914 German-Turkish Association. And he lobbied "the political establishment on the importance of Turkey in defending the Mediterranean against Soviet expansion" (Griffin 2009: 80; see Jaeckh 1960: 227 ss.).

Jaeckh summed up his self-perception of a lifetime "mission" as *Zivilapostel,* a one-man NGO (Jaeckh/Anshen 1951: 9-23; Jaeckh 1954: 8/9), when he wrote: "Wherever I was, I remained close to my Turkey, and wherever I operated, Turkey became an ally of the people among whom I lived – in Germany, England, and America" (Jaeckh 1954: 210). A more realistic way of putting how Jaeckh's lifelong turkophile narratives served him in his career might be that Jaeckh "was a man who knew how to sell himself and the Turks to a variety of audiences" (Griffin 2009: 81).

VIII

From *The War for Man's Soul* (1943) to *Weltsaat* (1960), Ernst Jaeckh's writings were calculated to persuade readers of his ostensibly unbending opposition to Nazism. However, Jaeckh also claimed to write the history of the German Political Studies Institute. In juggling with the facts of his biography, he was whitewashing a discipline. An apparent document, his testimony seemed conclusive proof that the study of politics and government in Weimar Germany had withstood the totalitarian temptation. As I have argued elsewhere (Eisfeld 1991: 99/100), it played a pivotal role by promoting, for several decades, the myth that, unlike other academic disciplines such as history or sociology, and unlike German society, German political science did not need to come to terms with the past.

In the United States, Jaeckh's influence on the discipline remained limited to fostering Middle East area studies at Columbia University. Always more propagandist and science organizer than scholar, Jaeckh left no visible imprint on American political science.

Arnold Wolfers' ingrained anticommunism, which had earlier contributed to his pro-Nazi stance, was ideally suited to the political climate during the 1950s and much of the following decade. If Hans J. Morgenthau's scholarly and public visibility vastly exceeded that of Wolfers, the latter' hidden influence deriving from his extensive advisory activities cannot presently be assessed, for Wolfers was also a secretive man: According to information provided by Yale University's Sterling Memorial Library, he destroyed the bulk of his correspondence on three occasions (1949, 1957, 1966).

In the mid-1960s, Wolfers was extolled by Roger Hilsman (formerly of the State Department, subsequently at Columbia University) and Robert C. Good (at the time of the State Department, later at Denver University) for "brilliantly combin[ing] the theoretical genius of Europe with the pragmatic genius of America, without succumbing to the banalities and excesses of either" (Hilsman/Good 1965: XI). The genius of Europe was hardly in evidence, when Wolfers' misread the Nazis' aims even after they had triggered World War II. And when the going in foreign policy would get tough during the Cold War, America's pragmatic genius tended to boil down for Wolfers, Hilsman and their likes to reshuffling instruments in the tool box, rather than questioning prevailing value assumptions. Wolfers' (and Hilsman's) opinions on U.S. interference in other countries, including military action, epitomise this aspect very well (Wolfers 1952: 227, 229; Hilsman 1965). The approach had major consequences, as any critical perusal of Robert McNamara's: *In Retrospect: The Tragedy and Lessons of Vietnam* (1995) is only too liable to show.

References

Anderson, Margret Lavinia (2007): " 'Down in Turkey, far away': Human Rights, the Armenian Massacres, and Orientalism in Wilhelmine Germany", *Journal of Modern History* 79, No. 1, 80-111.

Beck, Hermann (2008): *The Fateful Alliance. German Conservatives and Nazis in 1933*, New York/Oxford: Berghahn.

Becker, Carl Heinrich (1919): *Kulturpolitische Aufgaben des Reiches*, Leipzig: Quelle & Meyer.

Brauweiler, Heinz (1932): *Denkschrift*, April 29, Stadtarchiv Mönchen-Gladbach, Nachlass Brauweiler (Bestand 13/15), No. 192.

Dabag, Mihran (2002): „Der Genozid an den Armeniern im Osmanischen Reich", in: Volkhard Knigge/Norbert Frei (eds.): *Verbrechen erinnern*, Munich: Beck, 33-55.

Deutsche Botschaft Washington (1934): Bericht an Auswärtiges Amt über Vortragstätigkeit von Prof. Dr. Wolfers, February 27, encl. to: Brief Auswärtiges Amt an Reichsministerium für Volksaufklärung und Propaganda, March 24, 1934, ZStA Potsdam, REM No. 1445, 495.

Drechsler, Horst (1980): *Let Us Die Fighting. The Struggle of the Herero and Nama Against German Imperialism (1884-1915)*, London: Zed Press.

Eisfeld, Rainer (1991; [2rev]2013): *Ausgebürgert und doch angebräunt. Deutsche Politikwissenschaft 1920-1945*, Baden-Baden: Nomos.

Eisfeld, Rainer (1996): "German Political Science at the Crossroads: The Ambivalent Response to the 1933 Nazi Seizure of Power", in: Rainer Eisfeld/Michael Th. Greven/Hans Karl Rupp: *Political Science and Regime Change in 20th Century Germany*, New York: Nova, 17-53.

Fischer, Fritz (1969): *Krieg der Illusionen*, Düsseldorf: Droste.

Goltz, Hermann (2002): „Fünf weitere Dokumente aus dem Dr. Johannes Lepsius-Archiv Halle", in: Hans-Lukas Kaiser (ed.): *Die armenische Frage und die Schweiz (1896-1923)*, Zurich: Chronos, 355-368.

Griffin, George (2009): *Ernst Jäckh and the Search for German Cultural Hegemony in the Ottoman Empire*, MA Thesis Bowling Green State University, https:// etd.ohiolink.edu/ap/0?0:APPLICATION_PROCESS%3DDOWNLOAD_ETD_SUB _DOC_ACCNUM:::F1501_ID:bgsu1245518955%2Cattachment (accessed 12/27/ 2013).

Halberstam, David (1992): *The Best and the Brightest*, 20th Anniversary Edition, New York: Ballantine Books.

Heuß, Theodor (1921): „Denkschrift zur Errichtung einer Deutschen Hochschule für Politik", in: *Politische Bildung. Wille/Wesen/Ziel/Weg*, Berlin: Deutsche Verlags-Gesellschaft, 33-37.

Heuß, Theodor (1929): „Die Deutsche Demokratische Partei", in: Bernhard Harms (ed.): *Volk und Reich der Deutschen*, Vol. 2, Berlin: Hobbing, 104-121.

Hilsman, Roger (1965): "Orchestrating the Instrumentalities: The Case of Southeast Asia", in: Roger Hilsman/Robert C. Good (eds.): *Foreign Policy in the Sixties: The Issues and the Instruments. Essays in Honor of Arnold Wolfers*, Baltimore: John Hopkins Press, 191-203.

Hilsman, Roger/Good, Robert C. (1965): "Introduction", in: Roger Hilsman/Robert C. Good (eds.): *Foreign Policy in the Sixties: The Issues and the Instruments. Essays in Honor of Arnold Wolfers*, Baltimore: John Hopkins Press, IX-XII.

Hull, Isabel V. (2005): *Absolute Destruction. Military Culture and the Practices of War in Imperial Germany*, Ithaca: Cornell University Press.

Jäckh, Ernst (1916): *Das größere Mitteleuropa*, Weimar: Kiepenheuer.

Jäckh, Ernst (1921):„Rede", in: *Politische Bildung. Wille/Wesen/Ziel/Weg*, Berlin: Deutsche Verlags-Gesellschaft, 31.

Jäckh, Ernst (1927): *The New Germany*, Oxford: Oxford University Press.

Jäckh, Ernst (1929): *Amerika und wir. Amerikanisch-deutsches Ideen-Bündnis*, Stuttgart: Deutsche Verlagsanstalt.

Jäckh, Ernst (1931c): "Sees Sign of New World Teamwork", *Cleveland Plain Dealer*, Nov.15, Columbia University, Ernst Jäckh Collection, box 24.

Jäckh, Ernst (1932a): Chapter I/II, in: Ernst Jäckh/Wolfgang Schwarz: *Die Politik Deutschlands im Völkerbund*, Genova: Libr. Kundig, 7-51.

Jäckh, Ernst (1932b): „Ideologisches zur Abrüstung", *Zeitschrift für Politik* 21, 784-794.

Jäckh, Ernst (1932c): "Germany Riding Out the Storm", *New York Times*, June 25, Rockefeller Archive Center (RAC), Record Group 1.1, Series 717 S, Folder 177.

Jäckh, Ernst (1933a): The Political Situation of Germany, Address, Royal Institute of International Affairs, London, Febr. 6, xeroxed MS., RAC, Record Group 1.1, Series 717 S, Folder 177.

Jäckh, Ernst (1933b): Opening Address, DHfP Course for Prussian Civil Servants, March 27, Zentrales Staatsarchiv (ZStA) Potsdam, REM No. 1445, 401.

Jäckh, Ernst (1933c): Letter to Hans Heinrich Lammers, March 24, ZStA Potsdam, RK No. 19850, 37.

Jäckh, Ernst (1933d): Letter to Reichskommissar Dr. Rust, Encl., April 1, ZStA Potsdam, REM No. 1445, 411.

Jäckh, Ernst (1933e): Letter to Hans Heinrich Lammers, April 16, ZStA Potsdam, RK No. 19850, 90/91.

Jäckh, Ernst (1933f): Address, 6th Conference of Institutions for the Scientific Study of International Relations, London, June 1, RAC Record Group 1.1, Series 717 S, Folder 178.

Jäckh, Ernst [Jackh, Ernest] (1943): *The War for Man's Soul*, New York/Toronto: Farrar & Rinehart.

Jäckh, Ernst/Anshen, Ruth Nanda (1951): „Vorwort", in: Ernst Jäckh: *Amerika und wir 1926-1951*, Stuttgart: Deutsche Verlags-Anstalt, 9-23.

Jäckh, Ernst (1952): „Die ‚alte' Hochschule für Politik", in: Ernst Jäckh/Otto Suhr (Hrsg.): *Geschichte der Deutschen Hochschule für Politik*, Berlin: Gebr. Weiss, 5-32.

Jäckh, Ernst (1954): *Der goldene Pflug*, Stuttgart: Deutsche Verlags-Anstalt.

Jäckh, Ernst (1960): *Weltsaat*, Stuttgart: Deutsche Verlags-Anstalt.

Kennan, George F. (1983; [1]1967): *Memoirs 1925-1950*, New York: Pantheon Books.

Kloosterhuis, Jürgen (1994): *Friedliche Imperialisten. Deutsche Auslandsvereine und auswärtige Kulturpolitik1906-1918*, 2 Bde., Frankfurt a. Main: Peter Lang.

Korenblat, Steven D. (1978): The Deutsche Hochschule für Politik. Public Affairs Institute for a New Germany, Diss. University of Chicago.

Korenblat, Steven D. (2008): "A School for the Republic? Cosmopolitans and Their Enemies at the Deutsche Hochschule für Politik, 1920-1933", in: Manfred Gangl (ed.): *Das Politische*, Frankfurt a. Main: Peter Lang, 97-138.

Mariaux, Franz (1932): *Nationale Außenpolitik*, Oldenburg: Stalling.

Martin, Laurence (1994): "Arnold Wolfers and the Anglo-American Tradition", in: Douglas T. Stuart/Stephen F. Szabo (eds.): *Discord and Collaboration in a New Europe: Essays in Honor of Arnold Wolfers*, Washington: John Hopkins University, 11-16.

McNamara, Robert S. (1995): *In Retrospect: The Tragedy and Lessons of Vietnam*, New York: Random House.

Mogk, Walter (1974): „Ernst Jäckh", *Neue Deutsche Biographie* 10, 264-267, online version (www.deutsche-biographie.de/pnd118711253.html).

Murray, Marian (1934): "Seeks to Enlist Wartime Spirit", Report (newspaper unidentified) on Arnold Wolfer's April 14 talk to the Connecticut Council of International Relations, April 15, clipping in: Yale University, Sterling Memorial Library, Manuscripts & Archives, Group 534 (Arnold O. Wolfers Papers), Box 1.

Naumann, Friedrich (1900): *Demokratie und Kaisertum*, Berlin: Buchverlag der „Hilfe".

Nitze, Paul H. (1994): "Foreword", in: Douglas T. Stuart/Stephen F. Szabo (eds.): *Discord and Collaboration in a New Europe: Essays in Honor of Arnold Wolfers*, Washington: John Hopkins University, V-VI.

Politisches Kolleg (1922/23): Hochschule für Nationale Politik, *Vorlesungsverzeichnis*.

Sickle, J. Van (1933): Memorandum, July 18, RAC, Record Group 1.1, Series 717S, Folder 178.

Stuart, Douglas T. (1994): "Discord and Collaboration: The Enduring Insights of Arnold Wolfers", in: Stuart, Douglas T./Stephen F. Szabo (eds.): *Discord and Collaboration in a New Europe. Essays in Honor of Arnold Wolfers*, Washington: John Hopkins University, 3-9.

Strauss, Herbert A./Röder, Werner (eds.): *International Biographical Dictionary of Central European Emigrés 1933-1945*, Vol. II, Part 2, Munich/New York/London/Paris 1983.

Szabo, Stephen F. (1994): "Conclusion: Wolfers and Europe Today", in: Stuart, Douglas T./Stephen F. Szabo (eds.): *Discord and Collaboration in a New Europe.Essays in Honor of Arnold Wolfers*, Washington: John Hopkins University, 239-248.

Winks, Robin (1987): *Cloak and Gown. Scholars in America's Secret War*, New York: William Morrow.

Wolfers, Arnold (1925): „Amerikanische Demokratie. Versuch einer positiven Würdigung", *Blätter für religiösen Sozialismus* 6, January/March, 1-17.

Wolfers, Arnold (1932): "The Crisis of the Democratic Regime in Germany", *International Affairs* 11, 757-783.

Wolfers, Arnold (1933): "Hitler's Foreign Policy", *Yale Alumni Weekly* LIII No. 8, Nov. 17, 188 (Yale University, Sterling Memorial Library, Manuscripts & Archives, Group 634 (Arnold O. Wolfers Papers), Box 4).

Wolfers, Arnold (1940): *Britain and France Between Two Wars*, New York: Harcourt, Brace & Co.

Wolfers, Arnold (1962): *Discord and Collaboration. Essays on International Politics*, Baltimore: John Hopkins University Press.

Peenemünde: Challenging the Myth of NonpoliticalTechnology

*Since the mid-1980s, the term "reactionary modernism", coined at the time by Jeffrey Herf, has won wide acceptance among historians and social scientists. It denotes a combination – characteristic for both the Weimar Republic's political Right and for National Socialism – of extolling robust technical progress, while repudiating modern society and pluralist democracy in favor of "community" and authoritarian rule. In my 1996 study Mondsüchtig [Moonstruck] on the involvement of Wernher von Braun and other leading Peenemünde engineers in the Nazis' slave labor program for mass-producing the V-2, I used the notion to explain the engineers' attitudes and actions: They had been accepting, even promoting the assembly of a vehicle that was supposed to symbolize the **future**, by workers reduced to the status of peons (and worse) of the **past**. In the following paper, I attempted to combine Herf's concept with Norbert Elias' hypotheses (explained by him in The Civilizing Process and The Germans) on the long-term (non-)evolution, through political and social processes, of internalized self-restraint. I am indebted to Jeffrey Herf for his invitation in 2007 to discuss the approach at the University of Maryland's History Department.*

Peenemünde, the V-2 and the Exploitation of Slave Labor. A Study in Reactionary Modernism

I

To paraphrase John Lewis Gaddis' work on rethinking Cold War history:[1] *We now know.* We now know, for instance, that Walter Dornberger, former Commanding Officer of the Army Experimental Center Peenemünde, lied when he maintained in his 1952 memoirs that 'contradictory, confusing, and misleading' statements would be refuted and 'mistaken ideas ... correct(ed) ... once for all'.[2] An English translation of Dornberger's book, accordingly titled *V-2*, appeared two years later. In Germany, the book was reprinted three times during the 1950s.

The Peenemünde Army Center had offered the opportunity to Wernher von Braun and his team of engineers for developing the A-4 ballistic missile, better known by the label which Nazi propaganda provided: V-2, 'Vengeance Weapon 2'. Dornberger was anxious to leave his readers with the impression that the underground V-2 assembly plant, located near Nordhausen in the Harz mountains and code-named Mittelwerk (Central Works), had been a

---

1   John Lewis Gaddis, *We Now Know* (Oxford 1997).
2   Walter Dornberger, *V-2* (New York 1954), XV.

perfectly ordinary installation. Nowhere in his references to that facility – whether in its early stages as 'a new emergency factory still under construction' or, after completion, as the 'underground factory' whose assembly lines 'from August 1944 onward... produced six hundred rockets a month'[3] did he reveal that the plant had been built and missile production kept up by concentration camp inmates. Consequently, he also neglected to mention the Buchenwald subcamp named Dora[4], later expanded into camp Mittelbau, whose inmates were exploited as slave laborers.

Published in the same year, 1952, as Dornberger's memoirs, the small booklet *Bilanz* by Friedrich Kochheim, Mittelbau-Dora prisoner 21,549, contrasted with the former's whitewashing version in linking the concentration camp to the underground factory. Describing the combination of SS and civilian control over the detainees, Kochheim wrote he 'found it inconceivable that civilians worked in this place of horror and lived outside the camp, not divulging a word about the dreadful events that occurred here'.[5] His account provoked no response, aroused no public interest.

We now know that, along with Dornberger, former Peenemünde Technical Director Wernher von Braun[6], engineers of their entourage such as Dieter Huzel, Konrad Dannenberg and Ernst Stuhlinger[7], gullible biographers such as Eric Bergaust[8] and countless journalists[9] dissembled or were misled when they propounded what we may today term the Peenemünde legend. According to that convenient myth of the unspoiled rule of science at the Experimental Center, immune against Nazi temptations, neither von Braun nor his team were accomplices in the crimes of the so-called Third Reich. The establishment of a slave state for mass-producing the missile was either omitted or played down whenever possible ('The underground conditions of work were

3   Ibid., 111, 224, 241.
4   Already referred to by Eugen Kogon, *The Theory and Practice of Hell*, trans. Heinz Norden (New York 1950), 98.
5   Friedrich Kochheim, *Bilanz* (Hanover 1952), 57.
6   See Wernher von Braun, 'Reminiscences of German Rocketry', *Journal of the British Interplanetary Society*, 15 (1956), 125-145.
7   See, e.g., Dieter Huzel, *Peenemünde to Canaveral* (Englewood Cliffs 1962), 86, who waxed enthusiastically on the ‚spectacular' tunnels and assembly lines of the ‚gigantic' plant, without ever mentioning the adjacent concentration camp and slave labor; or, even three decades later, Konrad Dannenberg, *Introduction*, in Marsha Freeman, *How We Got to the Moon* (Washington 1993), XIII. Dannenberg, in charge of Project Design at the Peenemuende Army Experimental Center, later – in Huntsville – Project Director for the Jupiter IRBM, subsequently Saturn Systems Deputy Director, had joined the Nazi Party already on March 1, 1932 (No. 979,652). In contrast, Huzel emerged as a mere political 'fellow traveler' who had only become a Nazi Party member in 1933 (No. 3,230,173). See NSDAP Central Card File, Berlin Document Center (now Bundesarchiv Berlin-Lichterfelde).
8   Eric Bergaust, *Reaching for the Stars* (Garden City 1960).
9   See, e.g., Bernd Ruland, Wernher von Braun – Mein Leben für die Raumfahrt (Offenburg 1969).

unfavorable').[10] In any case, or so the legend insisted, that slave state had been exclusively run by the SS and had existed quite apart, both in geographical and in functional terms, from the morally intact world of the rocketeers.

Cold War realities provided the backdrop against which the Peenemünde myth could persist for more than three decades. In 1958, a modified Redstone tactical missile, christened Jupiter C and built by the selected team of former Peenemünde specialists shipped to the United States after World War II, launched America's first earth satellite, softening the Sputnik shock. By then, the times were long past when, in 1946, an article in *Life* Magazine had called Wernher von Braun simply another 'Nazi brain helping the United States'. A decade later, the same magazine referred to him as 'the seer of space'.[11]

After the Kennedy Administration's Bay of Pigs fiasco, the Cold War added one more element to the international struggle for power and prestige which would secure Wernher von Braun's rank as the symbol of Western spaceflight: the race to the moon. On July 21, 1969, an audience of millions watched the fuzzy, black-and-white television images which were transmitted from the lunar surface. Resembling apparitions, Neil Armstrong and Edwin Aldrin moved about in a murky landscape of strewn rocks and boulders, the first humans to have set foot on another world. Wernher von Braun and his group of engineers were the specialists who had built the Saturn V booster, the launch vehicle for the successful Apollo program, and they ranked foremost among those who reaped the laurels of that major achievement. Already by 1964, a West German weekly had introduced its readers to 'The Age of Wernher von Braun'.[12]

This chapter will first, and very briefly, trace how the Peenemünde myth was, by steps, shattered during the past two decades. Subsequently, the question will be pursued why numerous engineers, including Wernher von Braun, with little apparent qualms, came to in part initiate, in part support, in part accept the exploitation of concentration camp labor for their project's purposes, allowing themselves to get ever more deeply implicated in one of the most vicious Nazi policies.

John Cornwell has argued that, under the Nazi regime, pressures of competition and dependence were exacerbated, while professional integrity was corrupted.[13] Michael Petersen has recently focused on group pressures among the Peenemünde engineers, creating a community of shared professional am-

---

10 Ernst Klee/Otto Merk, *Damals in Peenemünde* (Oldenburg/Hamburg 1963), 61. The book was translated into English as *The Birth of the Missile* (New York 1965).
11 Life, 21 (1946), Nos. 24, 49; Life, 43 (1957), Nos. 21,133.
12 *Bunte Illustrierte*, No. 14/1964, 6.
13 John Cornwell, *Hitler's Scientists*, London 2003, 15.

bitions, beliefs and fears, of complicity and callousness.[14] Such short-term developments certainly played a part. However, at the outset of the 1930s von Braun already subscribed to the opinion that the German republic was 'no good'.[15] Leading Peenemünde specialists, such as Arthur Rudolph, later Saturn V project Manager, or Konrad Dannenberg, subsequently Project Director the Jupiter IRBM, entered the Nazi Party as early as 1931/32; others rushed to join in 1933.

The article will therefore approach the issue by looking at what Paul Lawrence Rose, in his perceptive study of the 'Heisenberg problem' (largely analogous, it will be suggested here, to the 'von Braun problem'), referred to as that scientist's 'deep conditioning' by 'very powerful ... elements of German culture' – the internalization of long-standing norms generating, in their turn, a peculiarly German set of 'beliefs and values'.[16] When attempting to explore the exact quality and origin of these values, the article will, however, proceed along lines of inquiry different from those chosen by Rose. It will rather put to use the work done by Norbert Elias and others on the socio-psychological consequences of authoritarian nation-building from above. Discussing, as part and parcel of that heritage, the attitudes and behavior inherent in the pattern of 'reactionary modernism' – the marriage of sophisticated technology to illiberal socio-political concepts -, the article will finally pursue some implications of that pattern for the Peenemünde engineers' comportment under Nazism.

II

It took from 1947 to 1987 to destroy the Peenemünde myth. In 1947, fourteen SS guards, four inmate Kapos, and one civilian engineer – Central Works General Manager Georg Rickhey – were indicted in the Nordhausen War Crimes Case (United States v. Kurt Andrae et al.). As a guide to the trial which was held at Dachau, the prosecution staff had a 65-page booklet prepared and printed. After the sentences passed in the case had been reviewed, a similar brochure of some 90 pages was issued by the office of the Deputy Judge Advocate for War Crimes. Both compilations included brief overviews of the Mittelbau-Dora camp's origins, development and organisation, of the horrific initial working conditions, the disastrous hygienic and food situation

---

14   Michael Brian Petersen: *Missiles for the Fatherland. Peenemünde, National Socialism, and the V-2 Missile* (Cambridge 2009), 151/152.

15   Willy Ley: 'Correspondence – Count von Braun', *Journal of the British Interplanetary Society*, 6 (1947), 155.

16   Paul Lawrence Rose, *Heisenberg and the Nazi Atomic Bomb Project* (Berkeley/Los Angeles/London 1998), 237.

during the first and final months, the several liquidation transports to other camps, and the final murderous evacuation marches. From these early publications, it also emerged that V-2 production plants had originally been planned in Peenemünde, in Wiener Neustadt some 30 miles south of Vienna, and in Friedrichshafen on Lake Constance. After Allied air raids on the three sites in the summer of 1943, Hitler ordered missile assembly to be carried out underground. The new facility was to be located beneath the Kohnstein hill near Nordhausen.[17]

However, the two publications do not seem to have been disseminated widely. In any case, they made no lasting impact.[18] Until two Mittelbau-Dora Gestapo officers and an SS guard were tried by a German court in Essen two decades later, the issue of V-2 production by concentration camp labour all but disappeared from public awareness.

The Essen trial, which had commenced in 1968, was concluded by 1970.[19] During the same year, the first scholarly work on Mittelbau-Dora was published in a volume on the history of Nazi concentration camps. The 45-page chapter[20] by Manfred Bornemann and Martin Broszat (the latter would soon direct the renowned Munich Institute of Contemporary History) essentially confirmed the earlier war crimes trial account, including particulars on the establishment of numerous sub-camps during the "middle" period between March and October, 1944 aimed at realizing additional industrial relocation projects and culminating in the designation of the spreading complex as Nazi Germany's last independent concentration camp Mittelbau.

In 1975, Wernher von Braun's name – two years before his death – was finally linked to the Mittelwerk/Mittelbau-Dora atrocities by former French

---

17 See Prosecution Staff, Nordhausen War Crimes Case, *The 'Dora'-Nordhausen War Crimes Trial* (n. p. 1947), 7-15; Deputy Judge Advocate's Office (7708 War Crimes Group, European Command), *United States v. Kurt Andrae et al.: Review and Recommendations* (n. p. 1948), 3-30. For a more recent brief account of the trial, see Robert Sigel, *Im Interesse der Gerechtigkeit. Die Dachauer Kriegsverbrecherprozesse 1945-1948* (Frankfurt/New York 1992), 93-104.

18 The first study to use the data furnished by the two brochures seems to have been Rainer Eisfeld, ,Von Raumfahrtpionieren und Menschenschindern: Ein verdrängtes Kapitel der Technikentwicklung im Dritten Reich', in id./Ingo Mueller (eds.), *Gegen Barbarei. Essays Robert M. W. Kempner zu Ehren* (Frankfurt 1989), 206-238.

19 Two defendants were sentenced to jail terms. Proceedings against the third were discontinued for health reasons. He was the sole accused to be still alive 20 years later. See Jens-Christian Wagner, *Produktion des Todes. Das KZ Mittelbau-Dora* (Göttingen 2001), 570.

20 Manfred Bornemann/Martin Broszat: ,Das KL Dora-Mittelbau', in Hans Rothfels/Theodor Eschenburg (eds.), *Studien zur Geschichte der Konzentrationslager* (Stuttgart 1970), 155-198. The authors had access to the results of a research team (Laurent Demps/Goetz Dieckmann/Peter Hochmuth/Manfred Pautz/Reimar Riese) based at East Berlin's Humboldt University and directed by Walter Bartel.

prisoner Jean Michel, who had already testified at the Nordhausen War Crimes Trial:[21]

> The supreme fraud has been successful. Von Braun and Dornberger have perpetuated their lie: the hell that was Dora and the missile technology cannot and must not be connected... I claim that Dornberger, von Braun, Gröttrup and all those lumped together conveniently as ,the Peenemünde scientists', knew perfectly well what crimes were being perpetrated at Dora... I claim that ... the mass-production of a prototype which was far from ready necessitated a permanent contact between the researchers at Peenemünde and the executors at Dora.

The debate (which remained largely restricted to France) fizzled out again until 'the issue of Arthur Rudolph' came along, and that – from the viewpoint of NASA officials – 'was just awful'.[22] In 1978, the U.S. Congress amended the 1952 Immigration Act by providing for the deportation of individuals who, between 1933 and 1945, 'had ordered, incited, assisted or otherwise participated in the persecution of any person because of race, religion, national origin, or political opinion.' To track down such individuals and to institute denaturalization proceedings, an Office of Special Investigations (OSI) was established within the Justice Department's Criminal Division. In October 1982, OSI lawyers flew to San Jose to question Arthur Rudolph, who had earlier been awarded NASA's Distinguished Service Medal, and whose hand three American presidents had shaken. Rudolph admitted at having had 'some control over the use of forced laborers' and to have 'request(ed) more forced laborers'.[23] Rather than face deportation proceedings, he renounced his American citizenship and, in March 1984, returned to Germany where he settled in Hamburg.[24]

Rudolph's case prompted the first critical assessments, by investigative journalists, of U.S. postwar policies ('Project Paperclip') that had brought

---

21 Quoted from the English edition: Jean Michel, *Dora* (London 1979), 93, 97 (the original was published under the same title in Paris 1975; chapter 14 was headed 'Wernher von Braun'). For the debate it unleashed, and for Wernher von Braun's response, see Ernst Stuhlinger/Frederick I. Ordway, *Wernher von Braun – Crusader for Space,* Vol. 1 (Malabar 1994), 53.

22 Stuhlinger/Ordway, *Wernher von Braun,* 236.

23 Thomas Franklin (i. e. Hugh McInnish), *An American in Exile. The Story of Arthur Rudolph* (Huntsville 1987), 237.

24 When Rudolph attempted in 1990 to enter the United States, from which he had been barred, via Canada, he was turned back, and a Canadian court sustained the removal order: 'The applicant's admitted activities give reasonable grounds to believe that he was an active participant and accomplice in both war crimes („ill-treatment or deportation to slave labor ... of civilian population... ill-treatment of prisoners of war") and crimes against humanity („enslavement, deportation, and other inhuman acts committed against any civilian population")' (Federal Court of Appeal, *Louis Arthur H. Rudolph v. The Minister of Employment and Immigration – Judgment* (Ottawa, May 1, 1992), 8.) Rudolph died in 1996.

German specialists to the United States.[25] In two 'ground-breaking'[26] 1987 and 1989 studies, Austrian historians Florian Freund and Bertrand Perz were subsequently able to establish a document-based link connecting Arthur Rudolph – in his erstwhile capacity as technical director of the Peenemünde Pilot Assembly Plant – to the first requests for slave labor from the concentration camps (through the A-4 Special Committee created by the Armaments Ministry), *initiating* – along with Army Ordnance – the establishment of a concentration camp in Peenemünde.[27]

Beyond definitely proving that having resort to slave labor for missile assembly 'had not originated with the SS',[28] the evidence presented by Freund and Perz substantially implicated Wernher von Braun in the founding of further camps in Austria, related to subterranean facilities for V-2 engine-testing and for developing both the Wasserfall anti-aircraft missile and the A-9 advanced booster (Redl-Zipf, code-name Schlier; Ebensee, code-name Zement). Regarding Schlier, von Braun suggested in November, 1943 that '120 German specialists might be saved' by employing a sufficient number of prisoners. In the case of Zement, where Mauthausen camp inmates had already been arriving since November, construction plans were realized only after acceptance by von Braun.[29]

Focusing on Mittelwerk and Mittelbau-Dora, a further 1989 article[30] proved that Wernher von Braun had lied about the extent of his involvement with Mittelwerk/Mittelbau. While von Braun always maintained that his visits to the Mittelwerk merely had to do with 'technical problems' about the missile, he had participated in a May, 1944 meeting which discussed the deportation of French civilians – to be employed in the plant after 'they had been clad', i. e. put into prisoners' zebra-striped garb. (It would later emerge

---

25 Tom Bower, *The Paperclip Conspiray* (London 1987); Linda Hunt, *Secret Agenda* (New York 1991). For the ‚traditional‘ presentation, see James McGovern, *Crossbow and Overcast* (New York 1964) and Clarence G. Lasby, *Project Paperclip* (New York 1971); for a critical rejoinder to Bower, John Gimbel, „German Scientists, United States Denazification Policy, and the "Paperclip Conspiracy"‘, *International History Review,* 12 (1990), 441-465. Gimbel's *Science, Technology and Reparations: Exploitation and Plunder in Postwar Germany* (Stanford 1990) offers the most systematic exploration of related British and U.S. policies.
26 Michael J. Neufeld, 'Hitler, the V-2, and the Battle for Priority, 1939-1943', *Journal of Military History*, 57 (1993), 534 n. 61.
27 Florian Freund/Bertrand Perz, *Das KZ in der Serbenhalle* (Vienna 1987), 65-68, 70-73; Florian Freund, *Arbeitslager Zement. Das Konzentrationslager Ebensee und die Raketenrüstung*(Vienna 1989), 42-48.
28 Freund/Perz, *Das KZ*, 68; Freund, *Arbeitslager*, 46, 449.
29 Freund/Perz, *Das KZ*, 81, 85/86; *Freund, Arbeitslager*, 61/62, 63/64, 69 n. 48.
30 Eisfeld, ‚Von Raumfahrtpionieren‘, op. cit. (n. 18).

that Walter Dornberger had lied to the extent of perjuring himself in 1969 during the Essen trial, when he was interrogated under oath.)[31] Was there more? From a letter von Braun wrote in early August, 1944, we now know that he set foot into the Buchenwald concentration camp. Following a suggestion by Central Works Planning Director Albin Sawatzki 'to make use of the good technical education of various detainees' for 'additional development jobs', he selected 'several qualified prisoners and obtained their transfer to Mittelwerk'. Transfer to the Central Works meant, of course, transfer to Mittelbau-Dora.

The von Braun letter was discovered on microfilm by Michael J. Neufeld, curator at the National Air and Space Museum in Washington.[32] In his seminal 1995 monographic work on the German army's missile program, *The Rocket and the Reich*, Neufeld's judgment was unequivocal:[33]

> Von Braun became implicated more deeply than ever before in the exploitation of slave labor... It appears that the prisoners were only factors of production to von Braun and his engineers.

From a subsequent book-length study of Wernher von Braun's career before and after 1945,[34] the engineer emerged as a man whom a succession of army officers had taken under their wing (Generals Walter Dornberger, Holger N. Toftoy, and John B. Medaris) in their efforts to secure a leading role for the – either German or U.S. – army in missile development, and who was far from eager to join a civilian spaceflight agency, after NASA had been established by the U. S. Congress in 1958. A man who, without apparent qualms, had, straight away in 1946 carried on in 1946 where he had left before, submitting to U S. Army Ordnance the project of a nuclear-tipped V-2 designated 'Comet'.[35] A man who, in 1952/53, had argued in favor of not only building an orbital station as a launching platform for nuclear missiles – "the ultimate weapon", in his words -, but of threatening the Soviets with a preemptive

---

31   See Rainer Eisfeld, *Mondsüchtig. Wernher von Braun und die Geburt der Raumfahrt aus dem Geist der Barbarei* (Reinbek 1996), 19/20.

32   Neufeld quotes from the letter in his *The Rocket and the Reich* (New York/London/Toronto 1995), 228. The facsimile of a copy which he graciously provided is reproduced in Eisfeld, *Mondsüchtig*, 135/136.

33   Neufeld, The Rocket, 207/208. Neufeld's opinion paralleled the assessment in Eisfeld, 'Von Raumfahrtpionieren', 226: 'In considerations on missile assembly, whether by the SS or by the engineers, both [i. e. engines or gyros, and camp inmates] were included as mere „factors of production". In this sense, von Braun might, after all, even be correct when he asserted that discussions had always focused on "technical questions".'

34   Eisfeld, *Mondsüchtig*, op. cit. (n. 31).

35   U.S. Space & Rocket Center, Huntsville, Wernher von Braun Papers: Beschreibung der Fernrakete 'Comet'; draft of letter to Los Alamos Laboratory, Dr. J. R. Oppenheimer; letter to Chief of Ordnance, April 12, 1946.

strike, should they decide to develop their own Star Wars capability.[36] No von Braun biography had previously acknowledged the existence of such a concept – an ultimatum involving the risk of global nuclear conflict – that might have befitted Stanley Kubrick's Dr. Strangelove.

III

Arthur Rudolph joined the Nazi Party in 1931 (No. 562,007),[37] after the NSDAP had received 107 seats in the 1930 Reichstag elections, finishing second only to the Social Democrats. Later, he would explain his move in terms of expediency, noting that he was out of work and that, 'from a business point of view, my decision did not prove wrong... By the end of 1934, I found employment'.[38] An American interrogator put him down as '100% Nazi'.[39]

Wernher von Braun became a member of the Nazi Party in 1937 (No. 5,738,692). Three years later, he also joined the SS (No. 185,068), where he was promoted three times by Himmler, holding the rank of *Sturmbannführer* – equal to an army major – by mid-1943. The evidence is that he, too, was motivated by considerations of expediency.[40] A U.S. military intelligence report concluded that 'he may have been a mere opportunist'.[41]

Eberhard Rees, von Braun's deputy in Peenemünde, later in Huntsville, his successor for three years as Director of the George Marshall Spaceflight Center, joined the SA in 1933. Nobody seems to have inquired about his motives.

Because categories such as '100% Nazi' or 'mere opportunist' may involve random judgments, their explanatory value is small: The attitude displayed toward the fate of concentration camp inmates by a supposed oppor-

---

36 Wernher von Braun, *Space Superiority as a Means for Achieving World Peace*, Address before Dinner Meeting of Business Advisory Council (Washington, D. C., Sept. 17, 1952 (printed booklet), 2, 14, 17/18; id., 'Space Superiority as a Means for Achieving World Peace', *Ordnance*, 37 (1953), No. 197, 774/775. See Eisfeld, *Mondsüchtig*, 186-191, and also Michael Neufeld's recent article ' "Space Superiority": Wernher von Braun's Campaign for a Nuclear-Armed Space Station, 1946-1956', *Space Policy* 22 (2006), 52-62.
37 Berlin Document Center (now Bundesarchiv Berlin-Lichterfelde), NSDAP Central Card File (also for Wernher von Braun).
38 Arthur Rudolph, Statement of May 16, 1947, National Archives, Record Group 330. Joint Intelligence Objectives Agency (JIOA) NND 851044. See Eisfeld, 'Von Raumfahrtpionieren', 229.
39 For a facsimile of the interrogation report, see Bower, *Paperclip Conspiracy*, 135.
40 See Neufeld, *The Rocket*, 179.
41 Quoted in Bower, *Paperclip Conspiracy*, 332.

tunist could obviously be no less callous than the posture shown by someone considered an ardent ideological believer.

Again: Why did leading Peenemünde engineers – Nazis or not – compromise themselves with Hitler's regime to the extent of actively, not just passively, participating in the exploitation of slave laborers?

Wernher von Braun for one never revealed the extent of his involvement. Until his death, he insisted that he 'never knew what was happening in the concentration camps'.[42] Von Braun also admitted that 'personally, (he) had fared relatively well under totalitarianism'.[43] Beyond that, the explanation which he offered for his collaboration with the brown dictatorship tallied with the defense advanced by a scientist whose path inadvertently crossed von Braun's, even if the two men never met – Werner Heisenberg who played a leading role in the German atomic bomb project: In 1942, armaments minister Albert Speer, 'convinced that the project would make only a modest contribution to the war effort..., gave other projects – Wernher von Braun's rocket research in particular – top priority'.[44] After the war, Heisenberg maintained that, even if the 'leading scientists disliked the totalitarian system', they 'could not refuse,... as patriots who loved their country..., to work for the Government when called upon'.[45] Wernher von Braun argued no differently: 'In times of war, a man has to stand up for his country,... whether he approves of the government's politics or not'.[46] The thought that the potential outcome of a war of aggression might be considered not in terms of defeat, but of liberation from a vicious, inhuman regime does not seem to have entered both men's minds. In effect, they were saying that armed conflict entitled a dictatorship to the same loyalty as any democratic-republican government.

Science and War in Nazi Germany: That is also the constellation on which John Cornwell focused in his attempt at explaining the moral corruption of German researchers, among whom he expressly included Wernher von Braun and his associates. Determined to exploit scientific disciplines, the Nazis (as Cornwell argued) exacerbated the pressures of competition 'to be first with a discovery', while emphasizing loyalties to discipline, to the idea of military might, to the nation. They succeeded the more easily because, long before the war, professional integrity had already been corrupted 'by the need to survive, by the desire, in some cases, to thrive under a depraved regime'.[47]

---

42 As quoted by Arthur C. Clarke, *Astounding Days* (New York 1990), 184.
43 Von Braun, 'Why I Chose America', *American Magazine*, July 1952, 111.
44 David C. Cassidy, *Uncertainty. The Life and Science of Werner Heisenberg* (New York 1992), 456/457.
45 Quoted in Rose, *Heisenberg*, 33.
46 See Stuhlinger/Ordway, *Wernher von Braun*, XIII.
47 Cornwell, op. cit. (n. 13), 15.

In his study, Cornwell evaluated scientists as individuals, judging each single expert according to his comportment under Nazi rule. Michael Petersen opted for a different approach in his dissertation, addressing the group processes by which the missile engineers were forged into a close knit community where 'cooperation, not competition, ruled the day' – including cooperation with the regime's murderous policies. Emphasizing the cumulative effects of secrecy, National Socialist ideology, professional elitism, material benefits and immaterial rewards, Petersen depicted the final result as the creation of a consensual 'cultural environment in which the needs of the regime and the needs of the missile specialists were inseparably intertwined'.[48]

To repeat, short-term processes such as those singled out by Cornwell and Petersen should not be discounted. But is their explanatory value sufficient when it comes to understanding motives for the specialists' complicity in the exploitation of slave labor? Discussing the role played by National Socialist ideology, Petersen displayed a certain ambivalence. On the one hand, he stressed its primary importance, added by enforced secrecy, for ushering in what Petersen termed a 'toxic atmosphere'. On the other hand, he downplayed its role, insisting that it was 'only one factor among many at play in the facility'.[49]

As mentioned at the outset, I suggest that the question of long-established patterns of thinking which favored susceptibility to the Nazi rhetoric should enter into the argument. Doubtlessly, such susceptibility was further reinforced by formative experiences during the Weimar Republic. The unexpected defeat in the Great War, the Versailles Peace Treaty stipulating huge reparations, the cession of eastern and western territories, not least the army's drastic reduction were considered national humiliations far beyond the political right. The idea that 'Versailles', symbolizing the war's results, should be 'revised' in time penetrated 'nearly every field' of cultural or political activity.[50]

The Versailles Treaty had denied weapons such as planes, tanks, or heavy artillery to the German army. Increasingly pushing for rearmament from 1930, the *Reichswehr* chiefs, in particular the manipulative and influental Kurt von Schleicher, were determined to realize their aims by 'revising' not merely the treaty, but also the democratic Weimar Constitution. Schleicher and his coterie were working towards pushing aside parliament, securing a government permanently dependent on the aging President Paul von Hindenburg, neutralizing the Social Democrats, winning over the 'disciplined', 'soldierly' National Socialists.

48   Petersen, op. cit. (n. 14), 9, 249.
49   Ibid., 252, 253.
50   Michael Salewski, ‚Das Weimarer Revisionssyndrom‘, *Aus Politik und Zeitgeschichte*, B 2/ 1980,15,19.

Wernher von Braun was only too aware of these strategems when he went to work for the army. In late 1932, he was recruited by Ordnance officers aiming at the development of a ballistic missile. Under an army grant, he did graduate work at the University of Berlin – receiving his Ph. D. two years later -, while concurrently beginning to develop and test liquid propellant motors for Ordnance. He was the son of a Prussian *junker,* Magnus von Braun, whom the government had sacked as a senior civil servant in 1920 for having endorsed the Kapp-Putsch, that infamous rightist coup attempt only thwarted, in the end, by a general strike. Earlier in 1932, the elder von Braun had been appointed Minister of Agriculture in Franz von Papen's ultraconservative, anti-parliamentary administration – a government which, with Schleicher serving as Minister of the Army, openly sought to build a 'national dictatorship' and which, by seizing the Prussian government from the Social Democrats in a virtual coup d'état, abolished the last important republican bulwark.

In his memoirs, Magnus von Braun later maintained that von Papen's administration had been 'a cabinet of gentlemen', intent on 'replacing the worn and sterile parliamentary system by decent work, order, and legality'.[51] Duty and order, community and legality, but disdainful rejection of liberty and equality, party politics and interest-group conflict: Those were the ideas espoused by the political right in the campaign it was waging against the parliamentary republic. According to later space travel historian and *Verein für Raumschiffahrt* member Willy Ley, who emigrated to the United States in 1935, Wernher von Braun reflected his father's political views: 'The German Republic was no good and the Nazis ridiculous'.[52] When, however, those same Nazis, during the first months of 1933, demonstrated that they were anything but ridiculous, the conservative elites who had declared war on the republic, and who had believed they could easily 'contain' Hitler, made their peace with the National Socialists.

Despising the allegedly 'weak' democratic republic, longing for the powerful state – the criticism leveled at Werner Heisenberg after World War II applied as well to von Braun: 'An intense nationalist with the characteristic deference to the authorities in control of the nation.'[53] In his attempt to reconstruct Heisenberg's thinking, Paul Lawrence Rose has situated the development of the physicist's attitudes and behavior in the context of what might be termed Germany's peculiar cultural course – 'traditional German dispositions' and 'longstanding assumptions' amounting to a 'German frame of mind'. According to Rose, this mindset was developed by 'crucial figure(s) in the formation of modern German mentality and culture' and came to be internalized by Heisenberg and other outstanding German individuals of the

51   Magnus Freiherr von Braun, *Von Ostpreussen bis Texas* (Stollhamm 1955), 234, 244.
52   As in n. 15.
53   Cassidy, *Uncertainty*, 470.

20th century during their formative years.[54] Rose included Martin Luther's distinction between inner and outer freedom; 'entailing the need for obedience to secular power'; Immanuel Kant's redefinition of the Lutheran formula, implying that an individual might retain his moral autonomy, while forgoing resistance against the state's laws or actions; Hegel's glorification of the (Prussian) state as the highest expression of reason and morality; finally, Richard Wagner's equation of national and 'apolitical' stance.[55]

But had the individuals singled out by Rose actually been able to create, between themselves, such a set of cultural dispositions? Should the evolution of a 'frame of mind' not rather be presumed to have involved processes that went beyond intellectual history? In what analytical terms ought the widespread pattern of attitudes about state authority and the behavior resulting from them to be conceived? And why had that pattern caught on to such a remarkable extent?

IV

In the most recent volume of his monumental series on German social history, Hans-Ulrich Wehler, paralleling his earlier interpretations, stressed that 'both new and older special historical conditions continued to make themselves felt since the 1860s', defining 'a "special path" which Germany followed as the exception among Western civilized and industrialized nations... To be talking, historicistically and apologetically, of any number of "special paths" pursued by European societies, misses the dire need to explain the causes of the German catastrophe.'[56]

This statement needs to be qualified. As Gabriel Almond and Sidney Verba have reminded us, every nation-building process, including the establishment of cultural value-patterns, needs to be understood 'as the product of a series of encounters between modernization and traditionalism'.[57] In the sense that in every such process tradition and modernity are apt to merge in specific ways, particular societies will pursue special paths of socio-political and socio-cultural development.

Consider the case of the United States. Settlement of the continent proceeded through a succession of westward-extending frontiers whose initial communities were often weak, lacking state organizations able to exert a monopoly of legitimate physical violence 'from above'. In their place, group

---

54 Rose, *Heisenberg*, XVI, 227/228.
55 Rose, *Heisenberg*, 227-232.
56 Hans-Ulrich Wehler, *Deutsche Gesellschaftsgeschichte*, Vol. 4 (Munich 2003), XXI.
57 Gabriel A. Almond/Sidney Verba: *The Civic Culture* (Princeton [4]1972; [1]1963), 7.

('vigilante') and individual ('lone ranger') violence sprang up 'from below' and were interpreted, particularly by frontier elites, as a necessary instrument for the advancement of civilization.[58] Mythologizing such violence, over generations, as a redeeming force has produced a widespread attitude persisting into the present, among both elites and broader strata of American society, that progress could and should be achieved, against presumed domestic and international 'rogues', through resort to violence.[59]

The statement that America, in that sense, also followed a 'special path' of modernization would probably not have been questioned by British historians David Blackbourn, Geoff Eley and Richard Evans when they challenged the thesis of German history's peculiarities.[60] The point they made was that, rather than considering authoritarian continuities, 'it would be more useful to consider the consequences of German society's *embourgeoisement...* (and) the forms of bourgeois predominance in a society increasingly dominated by capitalism'.[61] Heinrich August Winkler responded ironically that in the dark of capitalism, all national cats seemed to be grey to his British colleagues.[62] More seriously, neither before nor after 1871 were the 'delayed nation's' ruling castes (the owners of the East-Elbian landed estates, the professional bureaucrats, and the military – both latter groups largely recruited from the former) prepared to accept parliamentary control. Even if a society with strong bourgeois features did indeed develop between 1871 and 1914, 'it never gained primacy politically. The system of rule remained distorted in

---

58   Two examples are Nathaniel Pitt Langford, Vigilante Days and Ways, Vol. 1 (Boston 1890), XX, XXIII, 448, 453, on the Bannack (Montana) Vigilance Committee; Miguel Otero, *My Life on the Frontier 1864-1882* (New York 1935), 13, on the Hays City (Kansas) Vigilance Committee. Otero later served as Governor of New Mexico Territory. For an overview, see Rainer Eisfeld, 'Die organisierte Gewalt "selbstloser Männer": Vigilantes in den Vereinigten Staaten', in id.: *Streitbare Politikwissenschaft* (Baden.-Baden 2006), 211-226.

59   Richard Slotkin has traced the development of the myth of the violent frontier as the site of the clash between savagery and civilization into "a set of symbols" providing patterns of identification and legitimization for present-day American society, guiding its collective perceptions of present and future courses of action. See his *Gunfighter Nation. The Myth of the Frontier in 20th Century America* (New York 1992), 4-7, 14, 24. For a case study, see Rainer Eisfeld: 'Myths and Realities of Frontier Violence: A Look at the Gunfighter Saga', in Sean Anderson/Gregory J. Howard (eds.): *Interrogating Popular Culture* (Albany 1998), 42-54.

60   David Blackbourn and Geoff Eley: The Peculiarities of German History. Bourgeois Society and Politics in *Nineteenth Century Germany* (Oxford 1984); David Eley: *From Unification to Nazism: Reinterpreting the German Past* (London 1986); Richard J. Evans: *Rethinking German History* (London 1987). The ensuing controversy has been summarized by Hans-Ulrich Wehler, *Deutsche Gesellschaftsgeschichte*, Vol. 3 (Munich 1995), esp. 461-486 and 1278-1295.

61   Eley, *From Unification*, 11.

62   Heinrich August Winkler: ,Der deutsche Sonderweg. Eine Nachlese', *Merkur* 35 (1981), 796.

favor of authoritarian forms... Middle class rule in the sense of the decisive voice in policy-making lived on as a mere pipe dream.'[63]

Not just in Prussia, but in most of the many fragmented territories resulting from the 1648 Peace Treaty, German society came to be shaped 'from above' by command and subordination, military force and police supervision during two and a half centuries, until the defeat of 1918. The orientation of the average citizen to the political system remained 'the orientation of the subject rather than that of the participant'.[64] According to Norbert Elias, that long-term experience, repeated through successive generations, had profound consequences with regard to beliefs and behavioral traditions. External constraints on individual behavior continued to be imposed by, and attitudes were adapted to, autocratic rule from above.[65] Individuals thus experienced only limited opportunities to replace *external* restraint by evolving, in a drawn-out learning process, *self*-constraint – a pattern of own, inner-directed standards conducive to comporting themselves in civilized ways.[66]

Rather, 'personality structure, conscience-formation and code of behavior had all become attuned' to an authoritarian form of regime. Even after national unification which, again, 'came about as a gift from above', and during subsequent rapid industrialization, 'the habit of being ruled from above remained virulent. The idea that one could lean on a superior authority... retained its force of attraction'. The change to non-authoritarian institutions after the defeat of 1918 hardly touched the pattern because, as Elias would argue, 'new social techniques and skills which make greater demands on people's independence and self-control' had not been sufficiently learned.[67]

There was another side to the same process. Germany had also experienced the fragmentation of the first *Reich,* extreme disunity accompanied by external powerlessness. The 'backwards-looking' ideal of the lost *Reich* was subsequently 'project(ed) ... into the future', and the idealized picture, according to Elias, became 'more divorced from reality' than in every other West-European country. Precisely because of that deep gulf, demands made in the name of the *Reich* 'as a focus for real actions' could be perceived as particularly absolute and uncompromising, even 'border(ing) on the holy'.[68]

After the undigested defeat of 1918 and the humiliating Versailles Treaty, broad segments of the population lived through a frustrating republican in-

---

63   Hans-Ulrich Wehler, *Deutsche Gesellschaftsgeschichte*, Vol. 3 (Munich 1995), 772, 1289.
64   Almond/Verba, op. cit., 429. The observation relates to West Germany's first decade (data for the study were gathered between 1958 and 1960). However, the authors explicitly refer to long-time authoritarian patterns in Germany (see ibid., 38), and the characterization most certainly holds true for the earlier periods under consideration here.
65   Norbert Elias, *The Germans* (New York 1996), 338.
66   See Norbert Elias, *The Civilizing Process* (Oxford/Cambridge 1994), 512.
67   See Elias, *The Germans*, 338/339, 340/341, 342.
68   See ibid., 319/320, 324, 328/329.

terlude they perceived as 'devoid of authority'.[69] A German-National attitude of frustration and aggression would resort to hate for the republic and those who stood for the republic as 'a basic incentive ... the last certainty which had remained.'[70] Consequently, the powerful state again came to be doubly exalted, and a 'high fantasy content' was projected onto the dreamt-of 'Third Reich'.[71] Once that deeply desired new *Reich* had been established and seemed on its way to achieve some of the promised new greatness, it also commenced, by steps, not just to permit, but actually to *demand* from its subjects the systematic degradation of those whom the Nazis labeled 'inferior', even 'subhuman' – certainly Jews, but also Poles, Russians, Slavs in general, Sinti and Roma, homosexuals, 'anti-social elements' – in the last instance anyone designated an enemy of the 'Aryan community'.

It would do well to recall here that 'negative integration', authoritatively branding political, religious and national minorities as 'ferments of decomposition and subversion', had already belonged among the firmly established manipulative strategies of the Bismarckian and Wilhelmine empire.[72] Virulently aggressive and intolerant, the Nazi regime's ideologically laden demands made men, as Eva Reichmann observed, 'regress to a pre-civilised, pre-social level'.[73]

In the light of long-nourished collective attitudes, such demands from above could come to be considered by many as particularly compulsive, particularly inescapable, increasingly so after the outbreak of the war. As emphasized most recently by Wehler, 'the Second World War's barbarization was not inavoidably caused by the fierceness of military struggles. Rather, it was first initiated, then decisively aggravated in consequence of the instructions and liquidation orders issued by the "Third Reich's" political leaders'[74]. With 'mutual reinforcement ... set(ting) in motion a specific form of group dynamics', these instructions could impress ever 'wider social circles' as 'self-evident', even 'normal', progressively 'paralys(ing) critical judgment'.[75] Participating in the shooting of more than 30,000 Polish Jews in November 1943, the 'ordinary men' of Reserve Police Battalion 101 would invoke the orders of a 'distant system of authority that was anything but weak'.[76]

69   Annelise Thimme, *Flucht in den Mythos* (Göttingen 1969), 141, 146.
70   Ibid., 148/149.
71   Elias, *The Germans*, 342.
72   See, e. g., Dieter Groh, *Negative Integration und revolutionärer Attentismus* (Frankfurt/ Berlin 1973), 17, 36, 48/49, for the Social Democrats; Martin Broszat, *Zweihundert Jahre deutsche Polenpolitik* (Frankfurt [3rev] 1981), 130, 147 for Catholics, Poles, and Danes.
73   Eva G. Reichmann, *Flucht in den Hass* (Frankfurt 1955), 232. The original appeared under the title Hostages *to Civilization* (London 1950).
74   Wehler, *Deutsche Gesellschaftsgeschichte*, Vol. 4 (Munich 2003), 878.
75   Elias, *The Germans*, 343/344.
76   Christopher R. *Browning, Ordinary Men. Reserve Police Battalion 101 and the Final Solution in Poland* (New York 1992), 142, 174.

Likewise, and additionally strengthened by the imprint of that reaction-ary-modernist ideology that will be discussed in the next section, such de-mands could provide precisely the licence which the most 'obsessed'[77] among Peenemünde's leading engineers needed to become active perpetra-tors in one of the Nazi period's most atrocious chapters. 'I knew that people were dying', Arthur Rudolph would admit much later, when confronted by OSI lawyers with starvation and maltreatment in the Mittelbau-Dora camp. 'Everybody knew it.'[78] Yet Rudolph continued to request more inmates for his labor pool. 'A great many of these detainees were terribly malnourished *(befanden sich in einem furchtbaren Ernährungszustand)*', Wernher von Braun would acknowledge in the 1960s. 'I do not want to, and I cannot, deny that in any way'.[79] His awareness did not preclude von Braun from traveling to Buchenwald Concentration Camp and selecting additional detainees.

In an escalating process, an increasing number of Germans resorted to barbaric behavior because, conditioned by a long autocratic tradition, their in-ternal constraints had remained rudimentary, while external constraints were successively stripped off by a dictatorship to which they surrendered emo-tionally because it had succeeded in usurping the unquestionable, compelling ideal of the *Reich:* That is the gist of Norbert Elias' reasoning. His argument touches, of course, on the debate triggered by Daniel Goldhagen whose study also focused on those 'ordinary' Germans who, as accomplices of the regime, were involved in the most appalling of many Nazi genocides – the destruc-tion of the European Jews by gas, mass shootings, and slave labor. Goldha-gen attempted to provide an explanation by resorting to a boundless hate of Jews which he claimed to be profoundly rooted in German history and which he termed 'eliminationist anti-Semitism'.[80]

Elimination was also accepted, even tacitly supported by engineers like Arthur Rudolph or Wernher von Braun who were actively involved in ex-ploiting camp inmates to produce their missile. Yet before the evacuation of Auschwitz and Gross-Rosen in early 1945, merely a very small minority of those being worked or maltreated in Mittelbau-Dora until they were perishing by the thousands from hunger, weakness, disease, beatings were of Jewish descent. About 1,300 Jews were brought to the camp in May and September, 1944; an estimated 5,000 more only arrived with the evacuation transports from the camps in the east. The large majority of the detainees, however, came from Poland, the Soviet Union, and France – the three nationalities which continued to account for two thirds of the camp population -, from 20

---

77 See Irmgard Gröttrup (wife of Peenemünde engineer Helmut Gröttrup), *Die Besessenen und die Mächtigen* (Stuttgart 1958).
78 Franklin, *An American in Exile*, Appendix A, 236/237.
79 Quoted in Ruland, *Wernher von Braun*, 237.
80 Daniel J. Goldhagen, *Hitler's Willing Executioners* (New York 1996), ch. 2.

Czechoslovakia, Belgium, or Italy. The victims also included German Sinti, Social Democrats, and Communists.[81]

Anti-Semitism could and most certainly did add its impact to the murderous effects of the authoritarian syndrome analysed by Elias. However, as noted early on by Ruth Bettina Birn in her devastating critique of Goldhagen's book, it was definitely not a necessary requirement.[82] It could be substituted by a rigorous determination to realize – for instance – a technical vision at any price. Such rigor, unbridled by humane considerations – internal constraints, in other words -, found its instruments in a political environment systematically encouraging the infliction of extreme violence on anyone ostracized as an enemy of the 'Third Reich'.

The validity of the approach proposed here may be demonstrated by discussing a further case striking the observer as even more horrendous than the Peenemünde specialists' involvement with the slave labor program. That case concerns the 'perfectly normal' company of Topf and Sons, located in the city of Erfurt, and in particular their senior engineer Kurt Prüfer. Topf and Sons and their engineering staff were builders of the Auschwitz incineration ovens where thousands upon thousands of corpses were continuously burnt after having been murdered in the gas chambers. They also supplied the ventilation systems for the death factories.[83]

The two Topf brothers, owners of the firm, and Prüfer joined the Nazi party in 1933, but did not further distinguish themselves as National Socialists. They were neither ardent believers nor rabid anti-Semites. Quite the contrary, they kept on their company's payroll both former card-carrying Communists and 'half Jews' in the Nazi terminology, who had already been subjected to harassment. Surviving documents show that the management and the company's experts designed and offered ovens for mass incineration at their own initiative, considered business relations with the SS in terms of an equal partnership, did not shy away from conflict, were not coerced. They knew the precise purpose of the technology which they were offering, which

81   For the figures, see Jens-Christian Wagner, *Produktion des Todes,* op. cit. (n. 19), 405, 648. In addition to Jean Michel's *Dora* (n. 21*),* a more recent French survivor's memoir is *Planet Dora* by Yves Béon (English edition: Boulder 1997, with an introduction by Michael J. Neufeld; German edition: Gerlingen 1999, with an afterword by Rainer Eisfeld).

82   See Ruth Bettina Birn: 'Revising the Holocaust', *Historical Journal,* 40 (1997), 195-209, both with regard to the maltreatment of slave laborers ('Jews were very often the object of the cruelty of guards, but so were gays, people wearing glasses, intellectuals, people with a disability, overweight people, and people who offered any type of resistance' – 205) and to the final death marches ('examples not cited by Goldhagen show that conditions on all these marches were very similar, including those with only non-Jewish inmates' – 206).

83   See (also for the following) Stiftung Gedenkstätten Buchenwald und Mittelbau-Dora (ed.), *The Engineers of the 'Final Solution'. Topf and Sons – Builders of the Auschwitz Ovens* (Weimar 2005), 5-9 (Volkhard Knigge, 'Introduction: "Innocent Ovens" '), 14/15, 19, 39, 43/44, 59/60, 72-75.

was tested by Prüfer and other engineers on the spot. The respective sales accounted for less than two per cent of the company's total turnover.

As in Peenemünde, personal benefits – such as bonuses, improvement of status, exemption from military service – did accrue to a number of individuals. The evidence, however, is that, again, two factors were decisive for the specialists' complicity in mass murder. One, extermination policies were willed by the highest unquestioned authority, the State. Two, technical challenges were involved which spurred the ambition of the engineers. Notably Kurt Prüfer, the key player, realized the opportunities to enhance his reputation. In early 1943, he submitted to the Auschwitz SS Central Construction Management a proposal to accelerate the mass murders: Because Zyklon B required certain minimum temperatures to develop its lethal effect, Prüfer suggested that the gas chambers be heated with waste from the incineration ovens. The proposal was adopted by the SS.

Prüfer was arrested by the Soviets after the war and sentenced to 25 years in a penal colony. He died in 1952. Of the two Topf brothers, one committed suicide to evade arrest, leaving a note saying that he had 'always been decent'. The other re-established the firm in the West. All three cast themselves in the role of victims; no one professed any feeling of guilt.

V

The attunement of political culture to authoritarian institutions identified by Elias and others left its imprint on a variety of ideological approaches to political and economic contexts. One conspicuous result which increasingly caught on during rapid industrialization after 1871 was the marriage of sophisticated technology to Germany's illiberal tradition – that 'mixture of robust modernity and dreams of the past' which Thomas Mann would identify as 'technological romanticism'.[84] Because robust modernity relates to technology, the dreams of the past to society and polity, the ideology's essence is best captured by Jeffrey Herf s term 'reactionary modernism'.[85] Here was a pattern of thinking deriving directly from the special path of political culture identified by Elias and others, an amalgam both attractive and fatal which would make a major part of the Weimar Republic's society, not least among the engineering profession, additionally open to the Nazi combination of ide-

---

84   Thomas Mann, 'Deutschland und die Deutschen' (U.S. Library of Congress Lecture, May 1945), in id., *Politische Schriften* und Reden, Vol. 3 (Frankfurt/Hamburg 1968), 174.
85   Jeffrey Herf, *Reactionary Modernism. Technology, Culture, and Politics in Weimar and the Third Reich* (Cambridge 1984).

ological appeals to *Führer-led* racial 'community' *(Volksgemeinschaft)* and actual technological innovation.

For the large majority of the Peenemünde engineers, as Wernher von Braun's chief scientist Ernst Stuhlinger would observe retrospectively, 'the omnipresence of an outstanding leader' – referring to von Braun – 'was probably the most important factor.[86] Even decades later, after the U.S. Army Ballistic Missile Agency's Development Branch had been transferred to NASA, named the Marshall Space Flight Center, and Wernher von Braun appointed director of the new facility, the organizational structure would remind a perceptive American observer of the relationship between a 'managerial lord' and his 'vassals' (the laboratory directors) in a quasi-feudal system. The author, William Stubno, would go on to identify that structure, so different from American approaches to management, as 'deeply rooted' in Prussianized Germany's historical and cultural past.[87]

The cultural tradition epitomized by the notion of reactionary modernism had thus left an imprint on the comportment of Wernher von Braun and his entourage that lasted well beyond 1945, when Thomas Mann first spoke of the peculiar combination in terms reminiscent of those which Stubno would later use. To better appreciate the attitude, a look at the novel *Woman in the Moon* may serve as a convenient approach – the story by Thea von Harbou which she and Fritz Lang made into a spectacular silent film, the box office hit of the 1929/30 movie season.[88] Hermann Oberth became involved in the film's production, Willy Ley waxed enthusiastically that 'a spaceflight movie by Fritz Lang, with Prof. Oberth as scientific adviser, made the mind boggle',[89] and *Verein für Raumschiffahrt* members, Ley himself, Klaus Riedel, Rudolf Nebel, Wernher von Braun would continue to narrate how they had been captivated by the breath-taking illusion of a German spaceship making the first trip to the moon.

In the novel, the astronauts spent their last evening before the technological achievement in an outdoor cafe by a lake, where colored lanterns glowed in the trees. Later, Wolfgang Helius, the rocket's designer and pilot, wandered through fields and meadows, happening upon a white-bearded, sprightly old vagabond who taught him a few things about life before going to sleep in a hay-loft. Meanwhile, Gustav, the little freckled boy who would be a stowaway in the spaceship, ran along many country roads on his way to the launch station, with grasshoppers chirping and a frog hopping into a creek. Everybody's fate, however, would eventually be decided when the giant met-

---

86   Stuhlinger/Ordway, *Wernher von Braun* (as in n. 57), 78.
87   William J. Stubno, 'The von Braun Rocket Team viewed as a Product of German Romanticism', *Journal of the British Interplanetary Society*, 35 (1982), 445/446, 447.
88   The English edition that has been used is Thea von Harbou, *The Girl in the Moon* (London 1930).
89   Willy Ley, *Vorstoss ins Weltall* (Vienna 1949), 151.

al ship beneath the brilliant floodlights of the concrete launch base would be hurled upward and outward by the force of its liquid fuel motors. That narrative turned out to be a volatile hybrid not just because technological breakthroughs were set in a pastoral imagery. In addition, the clock was turned back in the novel with regard to social roles: Helius' love Friede Velten felt and behaved 'like a shield-bearer to her master'. As perceived by his chauffeur Grotjahn, Helius himself equaled 'master and god'. Liberty and equality were thus abandoned in favor of clear-cut hierarchy; 'selfish' interest and social conflict were rejected.

Reactionary modernism, by its 'selective embrace of modernity',[90] allowed to reject the Weimar republic as 'no good' (Wernher von Braun's view, as will be recalled), but to promote a technological advance that would restore national power and might even result in a German spaceship – 'constructed by eternal Faustian seekers', as Joseph Goebbels' *Angriff* approvingly commented on *Woman in the Moon.*[91]

During the Weimar Republic, a phalanx of prominent right-wing writers, making an impact on a broad reading public, argued in favor of reactionary modernism. Arthur Moeller von den Bruck, Oswald Spengler, Ernst Jünger were extolling a style both 'monumental' – heroic, irresistibly regulating individual existences – and 'idyllic' – pastoral and unspoiled, 'true to the German soul'[92], 'the steely energy' of engineering achievements,[93] the 'total' mobilization of technological resources 'in a warlike spirit'.[94] In each case, vehement renunciation of liberal-pluralist society and polity went along with the eulogy on technological achievement.

National Socialist propaganda could build on these foundations. The modern-reactionary hybrid was translated by the Nazi regime into both sustained ideological campaigns and attempts at 'unleashing technology': On the one hand, the familiar mythology of blood and soil, an anti-urban bias, glorification of peasantry, extolment of specific womanly qualities (particularly motherhood), emphatical insistence on the patriarchal structure of farm, family and factory; on the other hand – initially aimed at waging *blitzkriege* in Europe, in the end at preventing imminent defeat – the realization of techno-

---

90 Herf, *Reactionary Modernism*, 7.
91 Quoted in Reinhold Keiner, *Thea von Harbou und der deutsche Film bis 1933* (Hildesheim/Aurich/New York 1984), 107. – While Fritz Lang (who was of Jewish ancestry on his mother's side) emigrated in 1933, Thea von Harbou went on to write more than two dozen screenplays until 1945. However, she only joined the Nazi party in 1940 (No. 8,015,334; see NSDAP Central Card File, Berlin Document Center, now Bundesarchiv Berlin-Lichterfelde), not in 1932, as alleged by Michael Töteberg, *Fritz Lang* (Reinbek 1985), 74.
92 Arthur Moeller van den Bruck, *Der Preussische Stil* (Berlin 1931), 147 ss., 172 ss.
93 Oswald Spengler, *Der Untergang des Abendlandes*, Vol. 2: *Welthistorische Perspektiven* (Munich 1924), 622.
94 Ernst Jünger, 'Die totale Mobilmachung', in id. (ed.), *Krieg und Krieger* (Berlin 1930), 26 and passim.

logically advanced projects, such as synthetic rubber and fuel, superhighways, dive bombers, finally electric submarines, jet fighters, the V-1 flying bomb and the V-2 missile.

However, even the supposed 'wonder weapons' of the final war years were deeply flawed, testimony to the desperate Nazi leadership's 'escape into an illusion' whose irrational character blanketed the 'bankruptcy of the concept' in terms of any rational strategic assessment.[95] Moreover, a missile that was supposed to symbolize, like no other Nazi project, a steppingstone into a technologically advanced future came to be assembled by laborers abused more ruthlessly than the slaves of a distant past. Hans Mommsen has rightly insisted that it would be 'abstruse to rate a political system as modernizing which increasingly depended on slave labor and on the spoliation of the occupied territories'.[96] The Nazi regime's reactionary-modernist amalgam explodes the contention according to which 'the experience of National Socialism proves that modernization may occur in a dictatorial system'.[97]

As regards the engineering profession, however, the Third Reich's reactionary-modernist penchant for grandiose projects was perfectly suited to first impress those who, like Wernher von Braun, might originally have found the Nazis 'ridiculous', and later to attenuate any qualms they might have felt about becoming involved in the regime's barbarous policies. Where inner-directed standards of civilized behavior were already fragmentary, reactionary modernism provided a perfect final addition for toppling the balance between humane and inhuman comportment.

References

Almond, Gabriel A./Verba, Sidney ([4]1972; [1]1963): *The Civic Culture,* Princeton
Bergaust, Eric (1960): *Reaching for the Star,* Garden City
Berlin Document Center (now Bundesarchiv Berlin-Lichterfelde), NSDAP Central Card File
Birn Ruth Bettina (1997): 'Revising the Holocaust', *Historical Journal,* 40, 195-209
Blackbourn, David/Eley, Geoff (1984): *The Peculiarities of German History. Bourgeois Society and Politics in Nineteenth Century Germany,* Oxford

---

95 Eisfeld, *Mondsüchtig,* 143 (for the first quote); Neufeld, *The Rocket,* 52 (for the second quote).

96 Hans Mommsen, 'Noch einmal: Nationalsozialismus und Modernisierung', *Geschichte und Gesellschaft* 21 (1995), 398; and see already Jens Alber, ‚Nationalsozialismus und Modernisierung‘, *Kölner Zeitschrift Soziologie und Sozialpsychologie,* 41 (1989), 364/365.

97 Rainer Zitelmann, 'Die totalitäre Seite der Moderne', in Michael Prinz/Rainer Zitelmann (eds.), *Nationalsozialismus und Modernisierung* (Darmstadt 1991), 9.

Bornemann, Manfred/Broszat, Martin ‚Das KL Dora-Mittelbau' (1970), in Hans Roth-
fels/Theodor Eschenburg (eds.), *Studien zur Geschichte der Konzentrationslager*,
Stuttgart, 155-198
Bower, Tom (1987): *The Paperclip Conspiray*, London
Broszat, Martin (³rev 1981): *Zweihundert Jahre deutsche Polenpolitik*, Frankfurt
Browning, Christopher R. (1992): *Ordinary Men. Reserve Police Battalion 101 and
the Final Solution in Poland*, New York
Bunte Illustrierte, No. 14/1964
Cassidy, David C. (1992): *Uncertainty. The Life and Science of Werner Heisenberg*,
New York
Clarke, Arthur C. (1990): *Astounding Days*, New York
Cornwell, John (2003): *Hitler's Scientists*, London
Dannenberg, Konrad (1993): *Introduction*, in Marsha Freeman, *How We Got to the
Moon*, Washington, XI-XIII
Deputy Judge Advocate's Office (7708 War Crimes Group, European Command)
(1948): *United States v. Kurt Andrae et al.: Review and Recommendations*, (n. p.
Dornberger, Walter (1954): *V-2*, New York
Eisfeld, Rainer (1989): Von Raumfahrtpionieren und Menschenschindern: Ein ver-
drängtes Kapitel der Technikentwicklung im Dritten Reich, in id./Ingo Mueller
(eds.), *Gegen Barbarei. Essays Robert M. W. Kempner zu Ehren*, Frankfurt, 206-
238.
Eisfeld, Rainer (1998): 'Myths and Realities of Frontier Violence: A Look at the Gunfighter Saga', in Anderson, Sean/Howard,Gregory J. (eds.): *Interrogating Popu-
lar Culture*, Albany, 42-54
Eisfeld, Rainer (1996): *Mondsüchtig. Wernher von Braun und die Geburt der Raum-
fahrt aus dem Geist der Barbarei*, Reinbek
Eisfeld, Rainer (2006): ‚Die organisierte Gewalt "selbstloser Männer": Vigilantes in
den Vereinigten Staaten', in id.: *Streitbare Politikwissenschaft*, Baden-Baden,
211-226
Eley, David (1986): *From Unification to Nazism: Reinterpreting the German Past*,
London
Elias, Norbert (1994): *The Civilizing Process*, Oxford/Cambridge
Elias, Norbert (1996): *The Germans*, New York
Evans, Richard J. (1987): *Rethinking German History*, London
Federal Court of Appeal (1992): *Rudolph, Louis Arthur H. v. The Minister of Em-
ployment and Immigration – Judgment*
Franklin, Thomas (i. e. Hugh McInnish) (1987): *An American in Exile. The Story of
Arthur Rudolph*, Huntsville
Freund, Florian/Perz, Bertrand (1987): *Das KZ in der Serbenhalle*, Vienna
Freund, Florian (1989): *Arbeitslager Zement. Das Konzentrationslager Ebensee und
die Raketenrüstung*, Vienna
Gaddis, John Lewis (1997): *We Now Know*, Oxford
Gimbel, John (1990): *Science, Technology and Reparations: Exploitation and Plun-
der in Postwar Germany*, Stanford
Gimbel, John (1990): "German Scientists, United States Denazification Policy, and
the 'Paperclip Conspiracy'", *International History Review*, 12, 441-465
Goldhagen, Daniel J. (1996): *Hitler's Willing Executioners*, New York

Groh, Dieter (1973): *Negative Integration und revolutionärer Attentismus*, Frankfurt/Berlin

Gröttrup, Irmgard (1958): *Die Besessenen und die Mächtigen*, Stuttgart

Herf, Jeffrey (1984): *Reactionary Modernism. Technology, Culture, and Politics in Weimar and the Third Reich*, Cambridge

Hunt,Linda (1991): *Secret Agenda*, New York

Huzel, Dieter (1962): *Peenemünde to Canaveral*, Englewood Cliffs

Jünger, Ernst, ‚Die totale Mobilmachung‘ (1930): in id. (ed.), *Krieg und Krieger*, Berlin, 9-30

Keiner, Reinhold (1984): *Thea von Harbou und der deutsche Film bis 1933*, Hildesheim/Aurich/New York

Klee, Ernst/Merk, Otto (1963): *Damals in Peenemünde*, Oldenburg/Hamburg

Kochheim, Friedrich (1952): *Bilanz*, Hanover

Kogon, Eugen (1950): *The Theory and Practice of Hell*, trans. Heinz Norden, New York

Langford, Nathaniel Pitt (1890): *Vigilante Days and Ways*, Vol. 1, Boston

Lasby,Clarence G. (1971): *Project Paperclip*, New York

Ley, Willy (1947): ‘Correspondence – Count von Braun’, *Journal of the British Interplanetary Society*, 6 155

Ley, Willy (1949): *Vorstoss ins Weltall*, Vienna

Life, 21 (1946), Nos. 24, 49

Life, 43 (1957), Nos. 21,133

Mann, Thomas (1968): ‚Deutschland und die Deutschen‘, in id., *Politische Schriften und Reden*, Vol. 3, Frankfurt/Hamburg

McGovern, James (1964): *Crossbow and Overcast*, New York

Michel, Jean (1979): *Dora*, London

Moeller van den Bruck, Arthur (1931): *Der Preussische Stil*, Berlin

National Archives, Record Group 330, Joint Intelligence Objectives Agency (JIOA) NND 851044

Neufeld, Michael J. (2006): “Space Superiority”: Wernher von Braun’s Campaign for a Nuclear-Armed Space Station, 1946-1956, *Space Policy* 22, 52-62

Neufeld, Michael J. (1993): ‘Hitler, the V-2, and the Battle for Priority, 1939-1943’, *Journal of Military History*, 57, 511-538

Neufeld, Michael J. (1995): *The Rocket and the Reich*, New York/London/Toronto

Otero, Miguel (1935): *My Life on the Frontier 1864-1882*, New York

Petersen, Michael Brian (2009): *Missiles for the Fatherland. Peenemünde, National Socialism, and the V-2 Missile*, Cambridge

Prosecution Staff (1947): Nordhausen War Crimes Case, *The 'Dora'-Nordhausen War Crimes Trial*, n. p.

Rose, Paul Lawrence (1998): *Heisenberg and the Nazi Atomic Bomb Project*, Berkeley/Los Angeles/London

Ruland, Bernd (1969): *Wernher von Braun – Mein Leben für die Raumfahrt*, Offenburg

Salewski, Michael (1980): ‚Das Weimarer Revisionssyndrom‘, *Aus Politik und Zeitgeschichte*, B 2, 14-25

Sigel, Robert (1992): *Im Interesse der Gerechtigkeit. Die Dachauer Kriegsverbrecherprozesse 1945-1948*, Frankfurt/New York

Slotkin, Richard (1992): *Gunfighter Nation. The Myth of the Frontier in 20th Century America*, New York

Spengler, Oswald (1924): *Der Untergang des Abendlandes, Vol. 2: Welthistorische Perspektiven*, Munich

Stiftung Gedenkstätten Buchenwald und Mittelbau-Dora (ed.) (2005): *The Engineers of the 'Final Solution'. Topf and Sons – Builders of the Auschwitz Ovens*, Weimar

Stubno, William J. (1982): 'The von Braun Rocket Team viewed as a Product of German Romanticism', *Journal of the British Interplanetary Society*, 35, 445-449

Stuhlinger, Ernst/Ordway,Frederick I. (1994): *Wernher von Braun – Crusader for Space*, Vol. 1, Malabar

Thimme, Annelise (1969): *Flucht in den Mythos*, Göttingen

Töteberg, Michael (1985): *Fritz Lang*, Reinbek

von Braun, Magnus (1955): *Von Ostpreussen bis Texas*, Stollhamm

Wernher von Braun Papers, U.S. Space & Rocket Center, Huntsville

von Braun, Wernher (1952): 'Why I Chose America', *American Magazine*, July, 111-115

von Braun, Wernher (1956): 'Reminiscences of German Rocketry', *Journal of the British Inter-planetary Society*, 15, 125-145

von Braun, Wernher (1952): *Space Superiority as a Means for Achieving World Peace*, Washington, D. C.; id. (1953), 'Space Superiority as a Means for Achieving World Peace', *Ordnance*, 37, No. 197, 770-775

von Harbou, Thea (1930): *The Girl in the Moon*, London

Wagner, Jens-Christian (2001): *Produktion des Todes. Das KZ Mittelbau-Dora*, Göttingen

Wehler, Hans-Ulrich (1995): *Deutsche Gesellschaftsgeschichte*, Vol. 3, Munich,

Wehler, Hans-Ulrich (2003): *Deutsche Gesellschaftsgeschichte*, Vol. 4, Munich

Winkler, Heinrich August (1981), ‚Der deutsche Sonderweg. Eine Nachlese', *Merkur* 35, 793-804

During the 1990s, archive-based studies proved that a concentration camp had existed at the Army Experimental Center Peenemünde from mid-June to mid-October, 1943. The 600 detainees had originally been intended to start mass-producing the A-4 (V-2) missile – contrary to the "Peenemünde myth" about a paradise of experts with no links to the SS Slave State. After the British air raid in August, the camp inmates were transported to the tunneling site for the underground Mittelwerk factory on October 13, 1943. Arthur Rudolph and Walter Dornberger had been mainly responsible for developing plans to request prisoners from the SS and use them as slave laborers; Wernher von Braun became involved after the air raid. What about the roles of other top engineers, particularly Eberhard Rees, von Braun's life-long deputy and eventual successor as director of the Marshall Space Center in Huntsville, who had helped propagate the "Peenemünde legend"? And did, after WW II, any dissenters emerge from the ranks of former Peenemünde engineers who were prepared to deconstruct the myth? The following article first appeared as part of a collection edited in 2014 by the Friedrich Ebert Foundation, depicting Peenemünde not as a technological wonderland, but as a place of both perpetrators and victims.

The Peenemünde Legend: Origins, Perpetuation, Demise

I

Closely enmeshed with the Nazi regime's operating procedures, the Peenemünde Army Experimental Center, during the eight years of its existence, developed into a microcosm of the "Third Reich". The facility's engineers included convinced Nazis, political fellow-travelers and opportunists, in addition to a majority for whom merely "the project" counted. "The project" implied developing a weapon for terrorizing civilian populations. The rocket's mass production fell to concentration camp inmates – first in the Peenemünde Pilot Assembly Plant, subsequently in the underground Central Works near Nordhausen. Last but not least, the Peenemünde leaders brought in the SS by currying favor with Heinrich Himmler, in the hope that he might stimulate Hitler's interest in missile development.[1]

---

1   For details, see the two studies bei Michael J. Neufeld: *The Rocket and the Reich*, New York: Free Press 1995, and by Rainer Eisfeld: *Mondsüchtig. Wernher von Braun und die Geburt der Raumfahrt aus dem Geist der Barbarei*, Reinbek: Rowohlt 1996 (Springe: zu Klampen [3]2012).

The "Peenemünde Myth", in contrast, depicted the Army Center as an idyllic world of sober-minded engineers, immune against ideological tempta- tion, "cradle of space travel", aloof from Hitler's despotic regime, functional- ly separate from the Central Works slave state run by the SS. It permitted the engineers to face themselves, the Allies, in the last instance history. It al- lowed German society to identify with an achievement on which even the su- perpowers had to fall back. The myth's function consisted in deception and glorification[2].

Foundations for the myth were laid in 1945 at Garmisch-Partenkirchen during the detention and interrogation, by American intelligence, of several hundred Peenemünde technicians. In his 1952 book titled *V-2 – The Shot into Space*, former Peenemünde commander Walter Dornberger would subse- quently spell out the myth for the public. The work was immediately picked up by an American publisher (Viking Press) and reprinted three times in Germany during the next six years.

At Garmisch-Partenkirchen, the "sworn community"[3] of experts which had originated in Peenemünde would again prove its effectiveness – "closely knit", according to U. S. interrogators, and "firmly controlled" by Dornberger and von Braun, if necessary under penalty of being excluded from an eventu- al transfer to the United States.[4] Aiming at "maintaining their positions" by "continuing the work to which they are devoted in a business deal with the United States", Dornberger and von Braun painted in the most tempting terms an "encompassing command of rocket technology". Military and civil- ian prospects were combined into the sort of promotional strategy that had al- ready worked in "selling" the Aggregat 4 (the later V-2). Questions regarding the abuse of detainees in the Central Works were deflected by emphasizing the responsibility of the SS. Otherwise, the Central Works' existence was downplayed as far as possible.

Dornberger's memoirs were written with the "editorial cooperation" of Franz Ludwig Neher.[5] They contained a mix of fiction and fact. Dornberger's

---

2 A comparatively recent, readily accessible version of the myth is Ernst Stuhlinger/Frederick I. Ordway III: *Wernher von Braun: Crusader for Space*, Malabar: Krieger 1994.

3 Ruland, Bernd: *Wernher von Braun – Mein Leben für die Raumfahrt*, Offenburg: Burda 21969, p. 277. On processes of enculturation and community-building at the Peenemünde Army Center, see Michael B. Petersen: *Missiles for the Fatherland*, Cambridge: Cambridge University Press 2009 (also further below).

4 See (also for the rest of the paragraph) Jessel, Walter: *Special Screening Report*, Headquar- ters 3rd US Army, Intelligence Center (Interrogation Section), June 12, 1945, Appendix A, pp. 1, 2; Osborne, Ralph M.: *Special Interrogation Report: Evidence of a Conspiracy Among Leading German OVERCAST Personnel*, ibid., Oct. 29, 1945, p. 2 and Appendix B; both in: National Archives, Record Group 260, Box 5.

5 Neher's assistance was acknowledged in the book's American translation: *V-2*, New York: Viking Press 1954, p. XVI (see also the original German version: *V-2 – Der Schuss ins Weltall*, Esslingen: Bechtle 1952, p. 4 ["redaktionelle Mitarbeit"]). The book's 1980 reissue

repeated overtures to Himmler, hoping to exploit his support for gaining access to Hitler, were omitted; the engineers "enlightened spirit" was starkly contrasted with the despotic regime's "lack of understanding". Not a single word was lost by Dornberger and Neher about the camp inmates' exploitation at the Central Works, nor were they less taciturn about the use of slave labor in Peenemünde.[6]

Neher (1896-1970) had written aviation novels during the 1930s and 1940s. From 1951-62, he was employed as a press officer by the German Society for Space Research. The Peenemünde myth with its falsehoods, omissions, dramatizations was, in part, a literary – Neher's literary – product.

After the deaths of von Braun (1977) and Dornberger (1980), surviving "old Peenemünders" – as they were wont to refer to themselves – continued to propagate the myth. They were spearheaded by Eberhard Rees (1908-1998), referred to as "the man behind Wernher von Braun", his deputy in Peenemünde, his successor in Huntsville. When Dornberger's memoirs were reissued in 1980 under a suitably modified title in keeping with the times (*Peenemünde – History of the V-Weapons*), Rees contributed a preface, writing that the book could

> ...to the present day justifiably labelled *the* seminal work, excelling as it does in ob-jectivity and factual account...What I have found so particularly fascinating in Dr. Dornberger's book... is the incredible courage which he... exhibited in conflicts about the rocket... during the most dire straits...Often, he stood quite alone in confronting the power

and the intrigues of munitions authorities and the SS.[7]

Archive-based studies on Peenemünde, the V-2, and Wernher von Braun published since the late 1980s have paid scant attention to Rees. A recent German-language biography, written by Volker Neipp, a Museum Director in Rees' native town Trossingen (Southern Germany), largely ignored the state of research on Peenemünde. At least Neipp conceded it was "...safe to assume that he [Rees] knows who builds the [Central Works'] tunnels, and who assembles the A-4."[8] Rees, however, not only knew about the Central Works. In the summer of 1943, he collaborated with Arthur Rudolph, on whose sug-

---

(see below, n. 6) lacks the reference. Neher is listed in, e. g., Wer ist wer?, Berlin: Arani-Verlag 1969/70, p. 905, and is discussed by Rottensteiner, Franz: „Franz L. Neher (1896-1970)", in: Körber, Joachim (ed.): *Bibliographisches Lexikon der utopisch-phantastischen Literatur*, 9th Supplement, Meitingen: Corian 1987.

6   Dornberger's "subjective obfuscations" and "obvious omissions" were already criticized in an early study by Heinz Dieter Hölsken (published by the Munich Institute for Contemporary History): *Die V-Waffen. Entstehung, Propaganda, Kriegseinsatz*, Stuttgart: Deutsche Verlags-Anstalt 1984, p. 12.

7   Rees, Eberhard: „Preface", in: Dornberger, Walter: *Peenemünde – Geschichte der V-Waffen*, Esslingen: Bechtle 1981, p. 9.

8   Neipp, Volker: *Mit Schrauben und Bolzen auf den Mond*, Trossingen: Springer 2008, p. 34.

gestion, then request several hundred detainees were used at Peenemünde for preparing rocket production at the Pilot Assembly Plant. Twice Rees was put in charge of Rudolph during specific periods. And he attended the August 25, 1943 engineers' meeting chaired by von Braun, whose participants – after the British air raid on Peenemünde – recommended to continue exploiting the concentration camp inmates when production would be moved underground. The next section will discuss Rees' role in more detail.

In 1939, a supersonic wind tunnel had become operational at the Army Center, constructed under the direction of Rudolf Hermann (1905-1991), whom Dornberger had recruited from the University of Aachen. Hermann became a member of the Nazi Party in 1937 (No. 5,783,206). In 1941, he was promoted to the position of ideological instructor of the Peenemünde party chapter – a function whose German label (*Schulungsleiter*) he would realistically render as "indoctrination leader" in his sworn Paperclip statement of July 1947.[9] A young physicist stationed on the Russian front, Peter P. Wegener (1917-2008, a son of actor Paul Wegener) was ordered in 1943 to report to Peenemünde and to join the wind-tunnel staff, which meanwhile numbered 200. In early April 1945, Wegener briefly visited the Central Works to retrieve documents on supersonic aerodynamics. As he would write half a century later in his memoirs titled *The Peenemünde Wind Tunnels*, "this dramatic experience changed [his] early views of [his] stay at Peenemünde and became an essential part of [his] recollections."[10] Wegener not only described the harrowing picture which he had witnessed, attempting to reconstruct what he had felt at the time. In a chapter called "Looking back", he also discussed the literature on Project Paperclip and a number of documents on the involvement of Peenemünde's leading engineers in the exploitation of concentration camp labor, which had come to light during the 1980s and 1990s.[11] Wegener's memoirs have still not received the recognition which they richly deserve. The concluding section will look at them in more detail.

---

9   U.S. National Archives & Records Administration, Foreign Scientist Case Files, JIOA, Record Group 330, Folder "Hermann, Rudolf".
10   Wegener, Peter P.: *The Peenemünde Wind Tunnels. A Memoir*, New Haven/London: Yale University Press 1996, p. 160. A German translation: *Die Raketenforschung in Peenemünde*, Oldenburg: Schardt 2011, is not always reliable and also lacks Wegener's endnotes.
11   As Wegener notes both in his acknowledgments (pp. IX/X) and in the endnotes (pp. 181), we met in New York, discussing archival material which I had provided.

II

Eberhard Rees studied mechanical engineering in Stuttgart and Dresden from 1927 to 1934. On November 1, 1933,[12] he joined the SA (Storm Troopers) and was formally sworn in on June 20, 1934. His academic teacher, Enno Heidebroek, arranged for him to be employed by a Leipzig steel plant, a job at which the young graduate engineer attracted attention by his organizational skills and his meticulous work.[13] Heidebroek, whom Dornberger had recruited as von Braun's deputy and operations director for the development shops in late 1939, left Peenemünde already half a year later, after his wife had died. As his successor, he suggested Eberhard Rees.[14] Due to his pronounced aversion against standing in the limelight and his distinct practical bent, he would remain von Braun's deputy in Peenemünde and Huntsville for his entire professional career – save for the last three years (1970-1973), during which he succeeded him as director of NASA's Marshall Space Flight Center. In its obituary, the New York Times quoted Rees' answer to the question how he would describe his long partnership with von Braun as: "I have to do the dirty work."[15]

Since 1939, Army Ordnance (Weapons Testing Division, Group VI, *Ministerialrat* Godomar Schubert) had been pushing the establishment of a facility (*Fertigungsstelle Peenemünde,* FSP) for A-4 production, renamed Pilot Assembly Plant (*Versuchsserienwerk,* VW) in 1941. Arthur Rudolph – who had collaborated with rocketry pioneer Max Valier, had joined the Nazi Party in 1931 (No. 562,007), and in 1937 had accompanied Wernher von Braun from the Kummersdorf weapons range near Berlin to Peenemünde – was made the factory's technical director. At a meeting on September 8, 1941, von Braun, Rees and Rudolph agreed on rules of cooperation between the development and the assembly facilities.[16] The agreement assured that von Braun would be able, as technical director of the Army Experimental Center (*Heeresversuchsstelle Peenemünde,* HVP), to also exert decisive influence with regard to issues of production, viz.

---

12 Bundesarchiv Berlin (BArchB), ZA VI 0500 A 18 (former records of the Berlin Document Center, BDC), Central NSDAP Card File, SA Membership Card.

13 Neipp, *Schrauben,* p. 16.

14 See Fischer, Karin: „Heidebroek, Enno Wilhelm Tielko", in: Institut für Sächsische Geschichte und Volkskunde (ed.): *Sächsische Biografie,* http://saebi.isgv.de/biografie/Enno_Heidebroek_(1876-1955), accessed 2/15/2013; Neipp, *Schrauben,* pp. 17, 19/20.

15 „Eberhard Rees, Rocketry Pioneer, Dies at 89", *New York Times,* April 4, 1998, http://www.nytimes.com/1998/04/04/us/eberhard-rees-rocketry-pioneer-dies-at-89.html.

16 Bundesarchiv-Militärarchiv Freiburg (BArchF), RH 8/v. 1254 (Serien- und Massenfertigung A 4 1941-43), pp. 13-17.

that HVP as parent factory centrally steers preparations for replication (*Nachbau*) at FSP in the same manner as if FSP were any industrial replication factory.[17]

Peenemünde's leading designers later continued to maintain that development and production had been functionally separate. The agreement proves such allegations to have been merely convenient fiction. The fact that Rees, as von Braun's deputy, was twice during the summer of 1943 appointed "production czar" merely confirmed the arrangement.

After Armaments Minister Speer had created the A-4 Special Committee, headed by Gerhard Degenkolb, pressure on the Army Center increased dramatically, while ever more programs for missile mass production with increasingly unrealistic output rates began to circulate. On April 30, HVP Commander Leo Zanssen appointed Rees his special representative for 45 days, ordering him

> to adopt all appropriate measures for accelerating production start in FSP... During that period, he will continue to carry out his functions as operations director of the development shops... Dir. Rees is responsible to me that 20 A-4s will have been assembled... until 6/15/43. To carry out that special assignment, he is authorised to issue direct instructions to Director Rudolph and all other employees of the Pilot Assembly Plant. Dir. Rudolph has to support Mr. Rees in the fulfilment of his mandate in every manner.[18]

On April 16, 1943, Arthur Rudolph had recommended the use of concentration camp labor in producing the missile. On June 2, Rudolph, accompanied by two officers from Ordnance, presented a request for 1400 detainees – "on a preliminary basis" – to the A-4 Special Committee.[19] Because Rudolph was, at that moment, answerable to Rees, the latter must, at the very least, have been informed about the initiative, and must have given his assent. That would implicate Rees in the first decision to exploit slave labor in Peenemünde.

Zanssen's schedule proved unattainable. The first 200 prisoners from Buchenwald Concentration Camp arrived by mid-June, when Rees' special assignment was terminating. They had to construct an electrified barbed wire fence around assembly building F 1. The next 400 detainees followed in July, and prisoners started assembling rocket midsections.[20]

At an August 4 meeting, attended by Dornberger, Zanssen, Gerhard Degenkolb and his deputy Heinz Kunze, "the present EW Operations Director, Dipl.-Ing. Rees", was again appointed special representative, now "with dictatorial powers":[21]

---

17 Ibid., p 13.
18 BArchF, RH 8/v. 1254, p. 19.
19 For the details, see Eisfeld, *Mondsüchtig* (as in n. 1), pp. 89/90.
20 Ibid.
21 BArchF, RH 8/v. 1254, p. 143.

Acting upon special instructions, he will be fully responsible to the commander... for execution, in the EW, of the Degenkolb Program.

Rees was ordered

in consultation with Director Rudolph, Dipl.-Ing. Sawatzki and Dr. Thiel ... immediately to draw up a plan regarding manpower requirement for production and testing in VW... Submission to A-4 Special Committee by 20/8/43.[22]

In addition, it was resolved (according to the minutes, which bear Dornberger's signature):[23]

- Item 11: Missile manufacture would be entirely "carried out by convicts" (i. e. concen-tration camp detainees).
- Item 12: "For housing purposes, the first level of F 1" – the assembly building, where the detainees had already been temporarily put – would be made available to Rees. "At the earliest possible notice, the concentration camp inmates are to be moved to a barracks' camp on the empty space of the VW Administration Building."
- Item 14: The "assigned German reinforcement personnel... must suffice to... fill command positions in the fields of testing... and of assembly proper... The ratio of German workers to concentration camp inmates shall be 1 : 15, at the most 1 : 10... Implementation by HAP 11/ZP/PA[24] and Director Rees."

Rees was consequently implicated in plans for the further exploitation of concentration camp labor. The manpower requirement list which he, Arthur Rudolph, Albin Sawatzki and Walter Thiel had been ordered to draw up until August 20 has not yet been found. The British air raid on Peenemünde during the night of August 18 made Rees' appointment "with dictatorial powers" an issue of the past. Thiel was killed during the attack. Rees stayed in Peenemünde. Rudolph, as Operations Director, assumed the task of "setting up the [future] Central Works". Sawatzki was made the underground factory's Planning Director.[25]

Previously, however, on August 25, a gathering of senior engineers had met at Dornberger's instigation to discuss the envisaged move underground. The group consisted – according to the order recorded in the minutes – of Wernher von Braun (NSDAP 1937, SS 1940), Eberhrd Rees (SA 1933), Hans

---

22 Ibid.
23 BArch F, RH 8/v. 1254, p. 144.
24 By mid-1943, the Heeresanstalt Peenemünde had been code-named HAP 11, "Heimat-Artillerie-Park 11". "ZP" stands for "Zusammenbau-Planung" [Assembly Planning].
25 BArchF RH 8/v. 1210 (Chronik des Versuchsserienwerks Peenemünde, Vol. V: 1943), pp. 29, 30.

Maus, Karl Seidenstücker (NSDAP 1937), Erich Apel,[26] Artur Martin (again, NSDAP 1937), and Hans Lindenmayr. The engineers not merely debated issues such as awarding contracts for A-4 mass production, manufacturing component parts, or arranging for equipment and operational resources. They also envisaged the further "use" of the concentration camp prisoners already available at Peenemünde:

"The workforce for... manufacturing mid- and tail sections could be provided from theprisoners' camp F 1. German command personnel must be added."[27]

Rees might have been "liberally educated", his father on friendly terms with Theodor Heuss.[28] But the "community-building processes" at work in Peenemünde focused on the engineers' absolute commitment to their own – "technical" – priorities. Their "technological tunnel vision" included the "stunting of moral considerations" regarding slave labor, a "willing indifference" toward the suffering of the detainees.[29] Peenemünde eventually evolved into a replica of that "racist *Volksgemeinschaft*", into which the Nazi regime was transforming German society, and to whose institutions Michael Wildt has attributed the capacity for genocidal "practice without constraints" in occupied Europe.[30] Under a regime which encouraged the "dropping of barriers... to measures of gross inhumanity",[31] turning "rocket visions into reality" – as the *Huntsville Times* would eulogize Rees in its 1998 obituary – might readily include the resort to slave labor.

Rees would again closely cooperate with Arthur Rudolph in Huntsville during the Saturn moon rocket program. In the early 1980s, the U. S. Justice

---

26 In 1945, Erich Apel joined a group headed by guidance expert Helmut Groettrup, which was forcibly moved to the USSR in 1946 and established a new center for missile development on Gorodomlya Island in the Volga region between Moscow and Leningrad (for Apel's responsibilities, cf. the diagram drawn by Irmgard Gröttrup in: Albrecht, Ulrich et al.: *Die Spezialisten. Deutsche Naturwissenschaftler und Techniker in der Sowjetunion nach 1945*, Berlin: Dietz 1992, p. 99). Between 1951 and 1953, the engineers were successively allowed to return to Germany. Representing a non-ideological type of party official, Apel rose in the German Democratic Republic to the positions of Deputy *Ministerpräsident* and Chair of the National Planning Commission and came to play a prominent role in developing the "New Economic System of Planning and Management" (NÖSPL). When Walter Ulbricht in 1965, overruling Apel's stubborn resistance, accepted a new foreign trade agreement with the USSR that undid Apel's efforts at securing more flexibility in trade policy matters, the 48-year old Apel shot himself in his office with his service pistol.
27 BArchF RH 8/v. 1966 (Sonderausschuss A 4/Endabnahme 1943), p. 50281.
28 Cf. Neipp, *Mit Schrauben*, p. 13.
29 Cf. Petersen, *Missiles*, pp. 65/66, 80/81, 151, 200.
30 Cf. Wildt, Michael: *Generation des Unbedingten*, Hamburg: Hamburger Edition 2002, p. 858.
31 Kershaw, Ian: „"Working Towards the Führer", in: id./Moshe Lewin (eds.), *Stalinism and Nazism: Dictatorships in Comparison*, Cambridge: Cambridge University Press 1997, p. 102.

Department's Office of Special Investigations (OSI), established in 1979, advised Rudolph that it planned to prosecute him for crimes against humanity, intending to denaturalize him.[32] Rudolph renounced his United States citizenship and returned to Germany. In 1985, the Hamburg District Attorney's office instituted preliminary proceedings against him "on suspicion of complicity in the cruel killing of detainees".[33]

Both during the U. S. and the German proceedings, Rees testified in Rudolph's favor.[34] Rudolph was not, however, "eventually absolved of any war crimes", as contended by Rees' biographer.[35] Rather, the proceedings were closed in 1987 for lack of evidence of premeditated murder – the only offense not statute-barred, therefore still punishable, under German law. "On no account", as chief prosecutor Harald Duhn wrote to former Peenemünde guidance specialist Walter Haeussermann (now Huntsville), "can such proceedings result in a final positive exoneration, in the sense that Rudolph could, with certainty, not have been involved in such goings-on."[36] Notwithstanding that unequivocal legal statement, engineers and publicists (such as Neipp), in the United States[37] no less than in Germany, helped to spread a new obfuscating legend.

III

Disassociation from the "ancient Peenemünders" seems to have been an essential prerequisite for breaking with that tight-knit group's established narrative. Peter Wegener, whom Project Paperclip had brought to the U. S. in 1946, turned down several offers by Wernher von Braun to join his team. As he noted – "without any adverse judgment of the people involved" -, he had "wished to be independent of the group of German scientists and engineers that surrounded von Braun."[38] Recruited by the U. S. Navy, Wegener resumed his wind tunnel research at the Navy Ordnance Laboratory (Mary-

---

32 Evidently, it was not „the U. S. intelligence service" that wanted to strip Rudolph of his citizenship, as claimed by Neipp, *Mit Schrauben*, p. 139. A forteriori, that service was not in a position to "expel" Rudolph, as Neipp (ibid.) astonishingly writes.

33 Staatsanwaltschaft bei dem Landgericht Hamburg, Gesch.-Nr. 2100 Js 3/85 (Preliminary Proceedings against Arthur Rudolph), Vol. 15, pp. 2230, 2294.

34 Cf. Neipp, *Mit Schrauben*, p. 139.

35 Cf. Neipp, *Mit Schrauben*, pp. 139/140.

36 Staatsanwaltschaft (as in n. 32), Vol. 15, p. 2333.

37 Ward, Bob: *Dr. Space: The Life of Wernher von Braun*, Annapolis: Naval Institute Press 2005, p. 158. According to Ward, "the Bonn government", after having "investigate[d] Rudolph's wartime past,... absolved him of any war crimes". I have elsewhere discussed Ward's book in a critical review: *Journal of Military History* 70 (2006), pp. 1177-1178.

38 Wegener, *Wind Tunnels*, p. 53.

land), subsequently at the Jet Propulsion Laboratory in Pasadena. After having made contact with several universities, he joined Yale University as a full professor in 1960.

As briefly mentioned earlier, Wegener was a son of famous actor and director Paul Wegener (*The Student of Prague; The Golem*) from a third marriage. After receiving his Ph. D. degree, he was transferred in 1943 from the Eastern front to the Aerodynamics Institute in Peenemünde, where he worked under the direction of Rudolf Hermann at developing the first supersonic wind tunnel. In his memoir, Wegener described a political clash with Hermann in the summer of 1944; he left no doubt that the institute's director had supported the Nazi Party to the end. "All of us were careful in Hermann's presence."[39]

After the air raid on Peenemünde, the institute was moved to Kochel in Bavaria. In early April 1945, Wegener and another technical expert, both in army uniform, drove via Nordhausen to Niedersachswerfen where the Central Works were located. Provided with orders by von Braun, and having obtained special passes, they entered the underground factory to retrieve originals of their institute's research reports which had been stored there. The "largest group of workers", Wegener observed,

> comprised prisoners collected for the V-weapons project. They wore the striped uniforms and caps of inmates in a concentration camp... It was obvious to the laborers that we were uniformed outsiders, and they sneered at us in a somewhat unobtrusive way. I have never before experienced such glances of hate. Here I fall back on recollections recorded in the 1980s. There I wrote that I felt the only decent thing to do would be to rip off my uniform, put on a striped suit, and join the prisoners that all of us had put into such an inhuman situation. I have often tried to check these impressions of our visit, and I am certain about an overwhelming feeling of despair. We now tried to leave the tunnel as rapidly as we could.[40]

Even in retrospect, Wegener's depiction – obviously reflected several times since he made the experience – demonstrates how distraught he felt. About to exit the plant, he looked back and observed a change of shifts when "a dense stream of men in tattered striped uniforms was disgorged from the portal." Once again Wegener noted his emotional response: "I was frightened by this sight, and again we hurried on."[41]

However, Wegener did not confine himself to setting down his emotions. Following German unification, he twice, in 1992 and 1994, visited what was now the memorial site Mittelbau-Dora. He interviewed the staff and collected

39   Ibid., pp. 80/81, 82 (for the quote).
40   Ibid., p. 95.
41   Ibid., pp. 95/96.

the first archive-based studies which had started to appear.[42] The concluding chapter of his memoir, as well as the end notes, reflect that learning process, which had not reached its end by the time Wegener closed his recollections.

From the documents which he had seen at the time, Wegener drew the conclusion that only one person, Arthur Rudolph, was demonstrably guilty, though on a purely individual basis:

> This early [in April, 1943], quite voluntarily advanced, spontaneous idea of using prisoners, followed by the Mittelwerk action, sets Rudolph clearly apart from most others involved in the final mass production of the missile... No one else – to my knowledge – had suggested contacting the SS for a labor supply at Peenemünde... In sum, Rudolph's actions at the Mittelwerk demonstrate his personal guilt.[43]

As has now been established, Wegener erred. He continued to believe that Dornberger "had made every conceivable effort to keep the SS away" from Peenemünde.[44] And he also refused to assign any personal guilt to von Braun.[45] However, Wegener concluded his book pointing out that von Braun's August 15, 1944 letter to Albin Sawatzki, referring to his personal selection of detainees from Buchenwald for the Central Works, "poses more profound questions, none of which can be answered with certainty at the time."[46]

IV

Recent studies on Peenemünde have not drawn on Peter Wegener's memoirs to the extent which they would merit. That is the more unfortunate, as Wegener in passing does away with another part of the "Peenemünde Myth": He states categorically that, in Peenemünde, he "never heard a single remark about space flight", let alone about the A-4 as "a steppingstone toward a moon flight". Wegener emphasized that his statement included von Braun, who "never suggested this possibility, even in small social gatherings". In contrast, Wegener found it "amazing that the view of Peenemünde as the first space flight center could be discussed seriously in much of the postwar literature", and he explicitly ranked that notion a "myth".[47]

---

42   Ibid., p. 176 n. 3; pp. 180/181, n. 5, 6.
43   Ibid., p. 155.
44   Ibid., p. 155.
45   Ibid., p. 158.
46   Ibid., p. 182.
47   Ibid., pp. 41/42, 156.

Wegener's statement bears directly on the efforts of the "Project Team for a Technological Museum Wernher von Braun" [*Projektgruppe Technikmuseum WvB*] and the identically named association to downplay the missile's first successful launch in October 1942 as the mere "test flight... of an experimental Type A-4 vehicle". Purportedly, "a vehicle as a weapon" was never, "neither then nor later", launched from Peenemünde's Test Stand VII. Far from being "the cradle of space travel", as the project team contends on its website, that test stand, however, was the cradle of a terror weapon on which the Nazi leadership pinned its hopes: In March 1942, half a year before the October success, Walter Dornberger had bluntly advertised the rocket by promising that "rewarding targets such as London, industrial regions, port cities etc. [would] be taken under constant fire".[48]

Peter Wegener's ethical reflections, his determined attempts to check his recollections against the archival documents that have meanwhile come to light contrast visibly with the euphemistic portrayals by Dornberger, von Braun, Huzel, Dannenberg, Klee/Merk, Bergaust, Stuhlinger/Ordway, and others.[49] In many passages, Wegener's memoirs testify to that long-missed "work of mourning", of which it may be hoped that it will – late, but yet – finally pull the rug from under the "Peenemünde myth".

References

Bundesarchiv Berlin, NSDAP-Zentralkartei [*NSDAP Central Card File*]
Bundesarchiv-Militärarchiv Freiburg, RH 8 (Heereswaffenamt, Heeresversuchsanstalt Peenemünde)
National Archives, Record Group 260 (OMGUS, Field Information Agency, Technical, [FIAT])
National Archives, Record Group 330 (Joint Intelligence Objectives Agency, JIOA)
Staatsanwaltschaft bei dem Landgericht Hamburg, Gesch.-Nr. 2100 Js3/85 (Ermittlungsverfahren gegen Arthur Rudolph 1985-1987)
Albrecht, Ulrich u. a.: *Die Spezialisten. Deutsche Naturwissenschaftler und Techniker in der Sowjetunion nach 1945*, Berlin: Dietz 1992
Dornenberger, Walter: *V 2 – Der Schuss ins Weltall*, Esslingen: Bechtle 1952
Eisfeld, Rainer: *Mondsüchtig. Wernher von Braun und die Geburt der Raumfahrt aus dem Geist der Barbarei*, Reinbek: Rowohlt 1996 (Springe: zu Klampen ³2012)
Fischer, Karin: „*Heidebroek, Enno Wilhelm Tielko*", in: Institut für Sächsische Geschichte und Volkskunde (Hrsg.): *Sächsische Biografie*, http://saebi.isgv.de/biografie/Enno_Heidebroek_(1876-1955)
Herf, Jeffrey: *Reactionary Modernism*, Cambridge: 1984

---

48 Hölsken, *V-Waffen* (as in n. 6), p. 32.
49 See the preceding chapter's endnotes 6, 7, 8, and 10.

Hölsken, Heinz Dieter: *Die V-Waffen. Entstehung, Propaganda, Kriegseinsatz*, Stuttgart: Deutsche Verlags-Anstalt 1984

Huzel, Dieter K.: *Peenemünde to Canaveral*, Englewood Cliffs: Prentice Hall 1962

Kershaw, Ian: "'Working Towards the Führer': Reflections on the Nature of the Hitler Dictatorship", in: id./Moshe Lewin (eds.): Stalinism and Nazism: Dictatorships in comparison, Cambridge/New York: Cambridge University Press [5]2003, 88-106

Neipp, Volker: *Mit Schrauben und Bolzen auf den Mond*, Trossingen: Springer 2008

Neufeld, Michael J.: *The Rocket and the Reich*, New York: Free Press 1995

Petersen, Michael B.: *Missiles for the Fatherland. Peenemünde, National Socialism and the V-2 Missile*, Cambridge: Cambridge University Press 2009

Rees, Eberhard: „Geleitwort", in: Dornberger, Walter: *Peenemünde – Geschichte der V-Waffen*, Esslingen: Bechtle [4]1981, 7-9

Rottensteiner, Franz: „Franz L. Neher (1896-1970)", in: Körber, Joachim (Hrsg.): *Bibliographisches Lexikon der utopisch-phantastischen Literatur*, 9. Erg.-Lfg., Mettingen: Corian 1987

Ruland, Bernd: *Wernher von Braun – Mein Leben für die Raumfahrt*, Offenburg: Burda [2]1969

Ward, Bob: *Dr. Space. The Life of Wernher von Braun*, Annapolis: Naval Institute Press 2005

Wegener, Peter P.: *The Peenemünde Wind Tunnels. A Memoir*, New Haven/London: Yale University Press 1996

Wildt, Michael: *Generation des Unbedingten*, Hamburg: Hamburger Edition 2002

Sources

- "From Specialization to Teamwork: Current Challenges to Political Science", *Participation* Vol. 36 No. 1 (IPSA Bulletin, April 2012), 27-29
- "Political Science and Transition to Democracy: The German Experience", in: Anatoli Kruglashov (ed.): *Political and Sociological Studies*, Vol. XI: *Theory and History of Political Science: The Global and National Experience*, Chernivtsi: Bukrek 2012, 28-40
- "The 'Three Pillars of Hell' ": Hannah Arendt's Concept of Total Rule – Sources, Merits, Limits", Lecture, Conference in Memoriam Professor Ivan Prpic: "Conceptual Contestation and Political Change", Faculty of Political Science, University of Zagreb, November 7, 2014. First publication
- "Prospects of Pluralist Democracy in an Age of Economic Globalization and World-Wide Migration: A Tribute to Robert A. Dahl", Lecture, Faculty of Political Science, University of Zagreb, November 10, 2014. First publication
- "Klaus von Beyme: The Political Scientist as Global Scholar and Public Intellectual", *Participation* Vol. 37 No. 1 (IPSA Bulletin, May 2013), 13-14, reprinted in: *Klaus von Beyme. Pioneer in the Study of Political Theory and Comparative Politics*, Springer Briefs on Pioneers in Science and Practice, Vol. 14, Cham/Heidelberg: Springer 2014, V-VIII
- "Political Science in Great Britain and Germany: The Roles of LSE (the London School of Economics) and DHfP (the German Political Studies Institute)", *Polish Political Science Review (Polski Przeglad Politologiczny)* 2 (2014), No. 2, 71-82. The paper was originally read at the Conference: "Study and Research of Political Science in a Comparative Perspective", jointly held by the Consejo Mexicano de Investigación en Ciencia Política and IPSA RC 33, Mexico City, Nov. 7, 2013
- "From the Berlin Political Studies Institute to Columbia and Yale: Ernst Jaeckh and Arnold Wolfers", in: Felix Roesch (ed.): *Emigré Scholars and the Genesis of International Relations*, Basingstoke: Palgrave Macmillan, 2014, 113-131. Permission to republish is gratefully acknowledged
- "Peenemünde, the V-2 and the Exploitation of Slave Labor. A Study in Reactionary Modernism", Lecture, History Department, University of Maryland, April 16, 2007. First publication
- „Der ,Mythos Peenemünde': Entstehung, Verfestigung und erste Risse", in: Günther Jikeli/Frederic Werner (eds.): *Raketen und Zwangsarbeit in Peenemünde. Die Verantwortung der Erinnerung*, Schwerin: Friedrich Ebert-Stiftung 2014, 226-251 (author's translation; abridged)

About the author

Rainer Eisfeld was born in Berlin (1941). Educated at the Universities of Heidelberg, Saarbrücken and Frankfurt (Ph. D. 1971), he was Professor of Political Science at the University of Osnabrück, 1974-2006. Now emeritus.

International apppointments: Visiting Scholar, Center for European and Eurasian Studies, UCLA, 1995 and 2000; College of Social and Behavioral Sciences, University of Arizona, 2005. Visiting Professor, Department of Political Science, UCLA, 2002.

Professional activities: Member, International Conference Group on Modern Portugal, 1984-1989. Chair, IPSA Research Committee on Socio-Political Pluralism, 2000-2006. Member, IPSA Executive Committee (as Research Committee Representative), 2006-2012. Program Co-Chair, IPSA World Conference in Montreal: "International Political Science: New Theoretical and Regional Perspectives", 2008. Member, Board of Trustees, Concentration Camp Memorials Buchenwald and Mittelbau-Dora, 1994-.

Honors: Faculty Dissertation Award (University of Frankfurt), 1971. Volkswagen Foundation Research Grant (Akademie-Stipendium), 1989. Selection of *Mondsüchtig. Wernher von Braun und die Geburt der Raumfahrt aus dem Geist der Barbarei* by 'Bild der Wissenschaft' as one of the "Year's Outstanding Books on Science", 1997.

Books (international editions): Il pluralismo tra liberalismo e socialismo* (Bologna 1976); *Pluralizam između liberalizma i socijalizma* (Zagreb 1992); *Touha po měsíci. Wernher von Braun a zrození kosmických letů ze zvěrstev II. světové války* (Brno 1997).

Books (in English): *Political Science and Regime Change in 20th Century Germany*, New York 1999 (co-author); *Pluralism. Developments in the Theory and Practice of Democracy* (IPSA World of Political Science Series No. 4), Opladen/Farmington Hills 2006 (editor); *Political Science in Central-East Europe: Diversity and Convergence*, Opladen/Farmington Hills 2010 (co-editor); *Radical Approaches to Political Science*, Opladen/Toronto 2012.

Selected lectures: University of the Witwatersrand (Johannesburg) and University of the Western Cape (Capetown), 2003; Lecture Tour (supported by the German Research Foundation, DFG): Columbia University, University of Maryland and UCLA, 2007; Guest Lecturer, Moscow State Institute of International Relations – MGIMO University, 2008; Keynote Lecture, Conference on Political Science Development, Vilnius University, 2009; Universidad Iberoamericana (Mexico City), 2013.

Peer reviewer: Volkswagen Foundation, 1983-1993; *Political Studies*; *International Political Science Review*; *European Political Science*.

Find our journals on
www.budrich-journals.com

- Single article download
- Print + Online
- Subscription
- Free Content: ToCs, editorials, book reviews, open access content

Barbara Budrich Publishers
Stauffenbergstr. 7
51379 Leverkusen-Opladen

ph +49 (0)2171.344.594
fx +49 (0)2171.344.693
info@budrich-journals.com